THE EDUCATOR'S
GUIDE TO BUILDING
CHILD & FAMILY
RESILIENCE

MICHELE MYERS
& LINDA C. MAYES

To my daughters, Summer and Zoya. I admire the brilliant,
God-fearing young ladies you are. You face challenges with grace and faith.
To my mom, Sandra. You only want what's best for me.

—MM

To all the teachers who courageously did their best to care for their students
during the long months and years of the pandemic and who continue to give
their all to ensure a better future for children across the country.

—LCM

Senior Vice President and Publisher: Tara Welty
Editorial Director: Sarah Longhi
Development Team: Tonya Leslie, Raymond Coutu, Danny Miller, Shelley Griffin
Senior Editor: Shelley Griffin
Production Editor: Danny Miller
Creative Director: Tannaz Fassihi
Interior Designer: Maria Lilja
Editorial Assistant: Samantha Unger
Cover Illustration: Maurizio Campidelli

Photos ©: 26, 59, 87, 112, 149: FatCamera/Getty Images; 32, 41: PeopleImages/Getty Images;
48: Drazen_/Getty Images; 54: AJ_Watt/Getty Images; 89: Renata Angerami/Getty Images; 96:
Mint Images/Getty Images; 104: Sneksy/Getty Images; 108: andresr/Getty Images; 115: Goodboy
Picture Company/Getty Images; 122: Jose Luis Pelaez Inc./Getty Images; 146: David Johnson/
Getty Images; 147: Ahorica/Getty Images. All other photos © Shutterstock or © Scholastic Inc.

Credits: 19, 21, 23: "The Resilience Scale" © National Scientific Council on the Developing Child,
Center on the Developing Child at Harvard University. Adapted with permission of the Center
on the Developing Child at Harvard University and The Palix Foundation; 150: "Empathy Map"
courtesy of Dave Gray.
All rights reserved.

1 2 3 4 5 6 7 8 9 10   40   32 31 30 29 28 27 26 25 24 23

Scholastic Inc., 557 Broadway, New York, NY 10012

CONTENTS

ACKNOWLEDGMENTS

From Michele: I want to acknowledge the teachers (Sara Suber, Ali Jenkins, and Summer Myers) who willingly opened their classrooms for me to live and learn side by side for years. Your collegiality and honest collaboration made it easier to understand how resilience-informed teachers do this important work and do it well.

I want to acknowledge my friends/colleagues (Diamond Palmer, Richia Beaufort, Christie Martin, Eliza Braden, Margo Jackson, and Terrance McAdoo) who encouraged me throughout the process. I appreciate each of you.

Finally, I want to acknowledge the editorial team at Scholastic: Sarah Longhi, Tonya Leslie, Shelley Griffin, Karen Baicker, and Danny Miller. Your feedback and support throughout this process was essential in helping us create this timely work.

From Linda: All I learned about the science of resilience comes from my dear friend Dr. Steven Southwick who died in 2022 before he was able to read this book. I first want to acknowledge my gratitude to Steve for our many years of friendship and learning from one another. This book would also not be possible without Karen Baicker's ever-present friendship and wonderful ear for words and stories. She is my close Scholastic colleague, friend, and partner in the Yale-Scholastic Collaborative. Her voice is woven through this book. And finally, I also want to acknowledge the Scholastic team who brought this book to completion especially Sarah Longhi, Danny Miller, and Shelley Griffin among many others. My work with Scholastic has been career-changing and life-fulfilling. The Scholastic team is devoted to children flourishing throughout the world.

FOREWORD by LAUREN TARSHIS

I t's an honor for me to write the forward to this book, written by two people who have done so much to strengthen the lives of children, families, and educators. Dr. Michele Myers has spent years in classrooms training teachers and helping children overcome challenges so they can thrive as learners. Dr. Linda Mayes, the long-time leader of the world-renowned Yale Child Study Center, is a pioneer in the study of resilience. Linda is also a friend. During the darkest days of the pandemic, Linda's empathy, kindness, and practical wisdom made her a touchstone for me and many of my colleagues at Scholastic.

I am not a frontline warrior like these two amazing women. But, as the author of the I Survived book series, resilience has been a shaping theme of my work, too. In my historical fiction books, I delve into iconic events in history—World War II, 9/11, the Chicago Fire, Hurricane Katrina. I spend months researching each event and have traveled to almost every place I have written about.

Though my characters are fictional, each is inspired by real people I meet. Some I discover through diaries and letters and other firsthand accounts of long-ago events. But I also meet with survivors of more modern calamities—tornadoes, earthquakes, and wildfires.

Researching and writing my I Survived books takes months of hard work, and the writing (I'm sorry to admit) is for me often a grueling process. But I am deeply rewarded for my efforts through the connections I have made with kids, parents, librarians, and teachers from across the country. I especially love reading their emails and letters, like the one I received not too long ago, from a boy named Travis. "Dear Mrs. Tarshis," he wrote in thick purple magic marker. "Why do you write about things that are so *dupressing*?"

I smiled at the misspelling, but I pondered the question very seriously for days. Yes indeed, I thought, the topics I write about are *dupressing!* And yet I realized that somehow, spending more than a decade writing my disaster series has made me a more hopeful person than I was before.

Because over and over, I have discovered models of extraordinary resilience. Like Holly and Josh Fisher, whose beloved town of Paradise, California, was destroyed by a wildfire in 2018. Holly escaped with their two young kids while Josh, a firefighter, stayed behind to help battle the flames and save hundreds of lives. Afterward, they worked to support their community, create a temporary school, and rally support to rebuild the town.

Where does this kind of resilience come from?

This is the central question that Michele and Linda explore in this wonderful book. As they explain, resilience is not a mysterious force a lucky few are born with. Resilience springs from a set of capacities—the ability to forge close relationships, for example, and to help others. To find motivation and think in a nimble, flexible way. These and other "resilience capacities" can be learned, and teachers can play a critical role in nurturing these skills in the classroom.

And this book can be your guide. Beautifully written and packed with fresh insights, rich resources, and practical—*doable*—ideas, it shows how simple it can be to create a classroom that promotes resilience. Even before I finished reading it, I was making plans to send copies to every teacher I know and love.

The recent pandemic was a stark reminder that we can have no way of predicting what challenges are ahead for our children. But we can help them build the strength and flexibility they will need to cope with setbacks, disappointments, and loss—and to move forward with hope.

Thank you for all you are already doing for our children, and for your eagerness to do even more to help your students thrive in your classroom and beyond.

INTRODUCTION

As authors, we come to this work with our own histories that drove us to be fascinated by stories of resilience and driven to offer that capacity to others. We want to ground this book by sharing the inspiration that brought us each to become coauthors on this shared mission.

Michele's Story

We all have stories, and we all have experienced some form of trauma in our lives or know someone who has. I am no exception. When Linda and I began writing this book about resilience, I reflected on my life and thought about the events that have taught me important lessons about resilience. There

With my parents, Elijah and Sandra, my advisor, Dr. Amy Donnelly, and my beloved grandmother, Elouise, at my doctoral hooding. All of these people have helped me build resilience skills.

were many, but I thought of two major events that taught me the most. One happened in my personal life and the other in my professional work as an educator. Both had a profound impact on me and will forever shape how I engage in the world. What I am about to write requires vulnerability on my part and my trust that you, too, will garner important lessons as you read our book that will help you understand why resilience should be an essential element in teacher education.

On June 22, 1996, I stood before family and friends and vowed to love and cherish the man that I adored. During my marriage, I achieved great feats professionally, earning master's, education specialist, and doctoral degrees, and I advanced in my career. In my marriage, I experienced great joy, especially when I gave birth to our two amazing daughters, Summer and Zoya. But there were also traumatic events that occurred, both emotionally and physically. While confronting this trauma, there were many times that I felt overwhelmed, lost, and hopeless. But I knew I had two impressionable girls who needed me.

I am grateful that there were people in my network (my parents, grandparents, brother, aunts, friends, and the teachers with whom I worked) who rallied around me and helped in the ways that they could. I couldn't do it on my own, and I am glad that I did not have to. This was the first lesson I learned about resilience: Having a strong support system is critical. It was important for me to be able to tap into the relationships that I had with my support system and to know that they would do whatever was needed to help us. Another lesson that I learned is that it is okay to seek and receive help from others. Being vulnerable enough to say, "I need your help," and having someone say, "Don't worry, I got you," was very liberating. What I saw in my support system continues to impact me, both professionally and personally. This is especially true when working with children who are in crisis.

This brings me to the second event that enhanced my understanding of resilience. In my career, I have had the honor of working with countless learners, but there is one child who stands out for me. I will call her Latasha. I taught Latasha when she was in first and second grade. Latasha was a beautiful, energetic, and curious child. She had a smile that lit up any room. Her energy was positive, and all her classmates liked being around her. Latasha stole my heart with her sass and wit. It was a joy teaching and getting to know her.

However, when she came back for second grade, I witnessed drastic changes in Latasha's disposition. The smile that lit up our classroom was now replaced with deep sadness and despair. Her cheerful demeanor that everyone enjoyed had been replaced with a more withdrawn, and at times disruptive, little girl. I noticed other changes in her as well. She began pulling out her hair from the roots; she stopped eating lunch and was losing a lot of weight; and she began having loud outbursts. I knew something was not right, but I didn't know what.

I sought the help of the principal, guidance counselor, and social worker who monitored Latasha's placement in her new foster home. We worked together to get to the bottom of what was going on and eventually found out that Latasha was being sexually abused in her new placement. This discovery resulted in Latasha being removed from the foster home and admitted to a mental health facility to receive treatment for depression and trauma. I was devastated and blamed myself because I felt that I should have sought help for her sooner. My colleagues reassured me that I did my best by her, given what I knew at the time. I was only able to accept this and forgive myself after my first visit with Latasha at the mental health facility months later when I was permitted to visit her there. When I walked in, Latasha ran over and greeted me with a hug. I wept when Latasha said, "You are the only one who really loves me."

Like my divorce, this event helped me learn more about cultivating important resilience-promoting capacities in children. It taught me that identity matters. When I noticed changes in Latasha's behavior, instead of identifying her as a problem child and writing her up for each misbehavior, I remembered the little girl that I adored. I documented what I saw and sought others who were more skilled to help me figure out what was going on. This also helped me to grasp the importance of thinking more flexibly about a situation and being curious enough to get to the root of what was causing the change in behavior.

My experience with Latasha stayed with me and propelled me to do my best for all the children that I work with. Her words compel me to maintain that all children can benefit from resilience-promoting skills, not just the ones who have undergone some kind of trauma. She gave me purpose. It made me think of the traditional greeting of the fabled Maasai warriors: *Kasserian Ingera?* which means, "And how are the children?" The expected response is, "All the children are well," meaning that the children are protected and safe. The priority of the village is to make sure the children grow up in a healthy, loving environment where they can thrive. As a part of Latasha's village, I had done what was needed so that she could be well. And she is. I am happy to report that after receiving the help she needed, Latasha went to live with her biological aunt where she continues to thrive. I am also happy to share

With my daughters, Summer and Zoya

that my girls are thriving. Summer has a master's degree and teaches third grade, Zoya is a senior in college earning a bachelor's degree in business, and I, too, am doing well and thriving both personally and professionally. We each have learned resilience-promoting skills and strategies that are nurtured through our support

networks that help us to face life's challenges and move forward.

Linda's Story

Of all my experiences as a pediatrician on the front lines of acute pediatric care, the ones I had in the neonatal intensive care unit are etched most deeply and vividly in my memory. It is there where the combination of biology and a caring environment meet to make for literal survival and hope for a child. Two stories come together as one to shape my career-long interest in both the long reach of early adversity and the mystery of what gives some children a safe, sustaining buffer and others a very fragile, thin covering. Where does resilience take hold? What is resilience? One story is my first encounter with the smallest infant I had ever cared for.

Born too early and too small—barely a pound, this baby was a survivor. She was just over six months in her mother's womb before she came into the world, annealed like steel by the stresses of her mother's burdened life. We called her "Lunchbox," an affectionate nod to her small but sturdy presence just big enough for a lunchbox. Not like the large, feast-holding lunchboxes carried these days but the old style, small compact ones holding just enough to get its owner through the day. This was Lunchbox, making it through each day and keeping all of us going as other babies, sturdier by weight but frailer by constitution, struggled and sometimes succumbed around her.

Her isolette was just inside the door of the first nursery room. All of us walked past her isolette many times a day. We often gathered close to the door and spoke about the day's business but always with one eye toward Lunchbox. We imagined our constant presence made a difference for her. Lunchbox's isolette was an old-style box with portals that turned open with a click and a swish, allowing us quick access to the baby. Many a baby, conditioned to that sound, would start to move in agitation or turn away as much as their tiny muscles allowed but not Lunchbox. Instead, almost as if reaching toward the light and the world, we imagined Lunchbox was asking all of us, nurses, residents, fellows, and attending physicians alike, to care for her. With her family unable to travel the distance to see her often, we took her in. We cheered her every gained ounce, fretted over her few but concerning setbacks, and sometimes took extra time to sit by her bed just to give her company and find respite in her sturdiness. She was, after all, a miracle, the smallest baby of her birth weight and gestational age to survive and be doing so well.

To us, Lunchbox was an emerging individual with a personality and a growing book of stories about her spirit and strength. We all believed Lunchbox was simply determined to survive in this world, find whatever good that world had to offer, and we were there to help her on her way. Of course, we "knew" that Lunchbox was a fragile, delicate soul who needed our help even to survive, but it gave us all hope and strength to imagine Lunchbox as innately strong and beckoning us to care for her.

I was not there when Lunchbox was discharged home, but I knew we had sent her out into the world with the best odds our physical and emotional care could provide. Lunchbox would now be a middle-aged woman. Did she remain of small wiry stature, or did she fill out and have a body that matched what we were sure was her personality—forceful and determined, pulling the world in to help her? Did she grow into as sturdy and resolute a toddler and young child as we imagined her to be as a small, premature baby? Did she thrive in school? Did she find a loving partner, become a mother, become a grandmother?

It is these very questions about Lunchbox that bring me to the second story from my experiences in the intensive care nursery. As a part of my fellowship in neonatology, we also consulted in the clinic that saw formerly preterm infants now returning as school-aged children and adolescents so that we might understand the long-term impact of their early prematurity. Every family coming to that clinic asked these same questions—Will my child thrive in school, can he or she play sports, will he or she become a parent? But they also asked, not always on their first visit but after they got to know and trust us, could their child's lung disease of prematurity come back? Was there a chance he or she would become so seriously ill again? What could they do to protect their child against this and other unexpected tragedies that might lie ahead? As a physician in training, confident in the certainty of science, I initially found these more deeply felt questions puzzling, especially as I saw their healthy, robust, thriving sons and daughters.

But with more years and experience, I have come to see these parents were asking a much deeper question—how could they, as parents, give their children the best foundation and skills to meet whatever world they would meet? Fundamentally, this is what all of us caring for Lunchbox were trying to do. And this is what has brought me to the study of resilience and to working with Michele on this book.

My experiences in the neonatal intensive care nursery with Lunchbox and so many other small babies and their families have stayed with me for the rest of my career. They shape how I think about children's development, the possibility of recovery, growth, and gain, and especially about those capacities that help all of us face an often-challenging world. I continue to work with children and families but now am in the department of child and adolescent mental health at Yale and the Child Study Center. I came to Yale to do research so that I could better understand how to help the most vulnerable of children like Lunchbox reach their fullest potential. My research engaged families at the birth of their babies and followed them over now two and a half decades. What is clearest to me is we can all make a significant difference in children's lives by giving a safe, nurturing environment that gives them the chance to learn how to be caring, thoughtful adults themselves.

Individual differences abound in how all children develop and those individual differences combine with life's positive and negative experiences to make us who we are. But along the way, caring teachers, pediatricians, neighbors, parents, and relatives help us learn skills that promote our capacity to meet the inevitable challenges life brings our way. That is the purpose of this book—to help us all learn how to develop resilience-promoting skills among the children in our care.

We all want our children to have a strong, supportive village of caring people in place who will help nurture their capacities to meet life's adversities head-on. We want them to find opportunities in whatever challenges, hardships, and losses come their way. Our goal in writing this book is to offer the research, tools, and strategies to help you give the students in your classrooms the skills they need to foster resilience and a capacity to meet the inevitable challenges in their lives.

The Impact of Trauma and Adversity on Children and the Classroom

One important breakthrough in the field of education over the last several decades is a heightened awareness of the impact of trauma and adversity on the children who walk into our classrooms. Twenty years ago, few educators were talking about trauma, let alone considering it as they created their strategic plans and curricula. Today, most educators understand, broadly and deeply, the countless ways that children who have experienced adversity may have the deck stacked against them as they struggle to maintain balance while trying to learn, play, and connect to others.

Adverse Childhood Experiences (ACEs)

The term **Adverse Childhood Experiences** (ACEs) was first coined in the 1990s by the Centers for Disease Control and Prevention (CDC) and Kaiser Permanente in a study of the impact that traumatic events can have on children who experience them (Felitti, V. J., Anda, R. F., et al., 1998).

ACEs fall into three categories: abuse, neglect, and household dysfunction. Examples of ACEs include physical, emotional, or sexual abuse; neglect; parental separation or divorce; exposure to someone with a substance abuse problem or mental illness; and exposure to violence, among others.

ACEs can have a cumulative, long-lasting impact on an individual's physical and mental health (CDC Vitalsigns, 2019). As a group, individuals who have experienced multiple ACEs are at higher risk for chronic diseases, mental health disorders, substance abuse, and early mortality. Thus, addressing and preventing ACEs have been recognized as important public health priorities.

Still, the ACEs list is not comprehensive and other traumatic experiences can also have significant negative impacts on children's well-being. Moreover, the presence of ACEs does not necessarily determine an individual's future health outcomes, as resilience and protective factors can play a crucial role in mitigating the effects of trauma.

Over the past few decades, research has provided new information on the impact of trauma and sustained early adversity on children's developing brains (National Scientific Council on the Developing Child, 2020). We know that children's brains may become wired to respond acutely to any perceived stress. Children may have trouble paying attention and following directions, and they may act out in class. While these findings have challenging implications in the classroom, they reflect how children often adapt to their environments. This important science is increasing awareness among educators about the various ways trauma affects child development.

This awareness has also given rise to trauma-sensitive practices and approaches to teaching and learning. When educators implement these practices and approaches, they provide their students with a safe and supportive learning environment where children can learn the skills to lessen the emotional burden of trauma.

Creating a Resilience-Focused Classroom

In the wake of the pandemic, children are coming to school with levels of trauma, stress, and anxiety on a scale we have never seen. As an educator, you likely have your share of stressors in your life, too. You were drawn to this profession not only because of your desire to teach, but also because of your empathy and concern for children's well-being. In many cases, the emotional load of feeling incapable of helping a child who is struggling may also impact you negatively. Put simply, their trauma can become your trauma—by nature of your empathy. But take heart, the same coping skills and resilience strategies you develop in your students will also be helpful to you. We give you this book to spark a resilience-informed movement in education— practices and strategies that support children's capacities to thrive in the face of adversities, large and small.

Because studies (Walsh, 1996, 2003, 2006) document the positive influence of significant relationships on a child's resilience capacities, we also offer this book as a guide for building partnerships and support systems with families and communities. In your work with a child's family, you may speak explicitly to the skills you are trying to foster that promote resilience and emphasize that families can also support these skills. Many of the activities we give in the book are ones that families can do at home with children. We are convinced that our children will be stronger when we cultivate effective partnerships with families and communities that equip children with the skills to be more resourceful when dealing with the hardships that life may present.

We have developed a framework that we will revisit throughout the book to give you a structure for understanding the capacities and related skills we want students to develop and for communicating with and supporting families in fostering resilience. The framework provides a map of five key resilience-promoting capacities and ways to foster those capacities as you go about your day-to-day teaching:

1. Developing supportive relationships
2. Forming positive self-identities
3. Supporting curiosity and motivation
4. Engaging in flexible thinking
5. Demonstrating altruism

How to Navigate This Book

This book is for educators like you who want to help their students thrive in our ever-evolving world, equipped to deal with the challenges life will inevitably bring. It is organized to help you weave resilience skill-building into the daily life of your classroom. Chapter 1 takes a deep dive into resilience. Each chapter that follows focuses on one of the five resilience-promoting capacities that help ensure that all children are able to thrive.

Each chapter begins with a description of the capacity and key principles related to it. We then share actions that you can do in your classroom to help children develop that capacity. From there, we offer a section that details the negative outcomes a child might experience when he or she does not receive support or learn to respond to adversities and trauma. We also share how you can develop the capacity through your literacy instruction. We provide teacher-approved routines and activities for grades K–2 and 3–5 to help your students develop supportive relationships, form positive self-identities, build curiosity and motivation, engage in flexible thinking, and demonstrate altruism.

CHAPTER 1

WHAT IS RESILIENCE?

"Resiliency is something you do, more than something you have. You become highly resilient by continuously learning your best way of being yourself in your circumstance."

—Al Siebert

We believe that literacy can be used to foster resilience in children and families. As we've seen in our work with the Yale Child Study Center-Scholastic Collaborative for Child & Family Resilience, the more children learn about the world through stories and reading, the more opportunities they have to grow and flourish. It's a simple but profound link—literacy to resilience to better health.

As we look at the factors related to child and family resilience, we are focused on some of the same questions that you have:

- Why do some children seem to thrive despite adversity in their lives?
- Can we develop capacities among children for greater resilience?
- In what ways can educators, who aren't trained mental health professionals, help children and families cope with adversity?

YALE CHILD STUDY CENTER+SCHOLASTIC

COLLABORATIVE FOR **CHILD & FAMILY RESILIENCE**

The Yale Child Study Center-Scholastic Collaborative for Child & Family Resilience is a partnership with a mission—to give children the skills they need to flourish and reach their fullest potential. Researchers and medical professionals together with publishing teams develop literacy and health-based intervention resources for children and families to address developmental and mental health concerns. These two organizations are united in the firm belief that literacy promotes health and well-being.

The Resilience Scale

Many people imagine resilience as a rubber band—when we are stretched or stressed, we can bounce back. That metaphor assumes resilience resides within the individual person. It inherently puts the burden of that elasticity on the individual child or adult. The FrameWorks Institute and the Palix Foundation, consulting with Harvard's Center on the Developing Child, have introduced a metaphor that aptly conveys the principles of child resilience (National Scientific Council on the Developing Child, 2015). Their Resilience Scale model, adapted by the Palix Foundation, shows a scale with the child as the fulcrum in the middle.

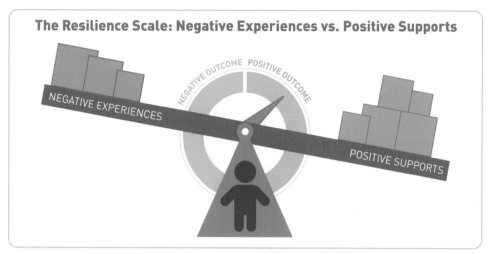

The Resilience Scale: Negative Experiences vs. Positive Supports

NEGATIVE OUTCOME POSITIVE OUTCOME

NEGATIVE EXPERIENCES

POSITIVE SUPPORTS

When children have more positive supports than negative experiences, they are more likely to experience positive outcomes. (Resilience Scale adapted with permission of the Palix Foundation)

Red Boxes: Negative Experiences

The red boxes on the left side of the scale represent negative experiences that can weigh on a child's life, tipping it toward negative outcomes. Think about the children in your classroom and some of the adverse circumstances they face in and out of school. The child who comes to school hungry. The child who has just moved homes… again. The child who may be experiencing bullying or witnessing violence at home. The negative experiences might include exposure to poverty or hunger or any of the Adverse Childhood Experiences (ACEs) that have been cataloged, such as individual or community violence, substance use at home, and homelessness. Or they might include the stress that COVID-19 has placed on their lives.

Green Boxes: Positive Supports

The green boxes on the right side of the scale represent the positive supports in a child's world, tipping the scale toward positive outcomes. Imagine again the children in your classroom. What keeps them going when they

Defining Resilience

Resilience is the ability to respond positively in the face of adversity. Children develop skills and capacities that help them become more resilient with the guidance of caring adults and other social supports. By cultivating safe and supportive relationships and resources and nurturing internal coping skills, we can create optimal conditions for children to weather life's adversities.

are facing challenges in their lives? What lifts them up when they are down? To whom and where can they go for help? These resources include caring relationships, healthy schools, and access to healthcare among many others. The more the scale is weighted toward the positive, the more the child is protected from the negative factors in his or her world.

As an educator, you can likely do little to remove the red boxes from the negative side of the scale. You can't single-handedly improve a child's out-of-school environment or cure an illness. But often, you can provide some of the counterbalancing green boxes on the positive side. Indeed, your caring attention and the classroom climate you foster can be a green box in and of itself. And even more often, one of the biggest green boxes you can provide is by being a positive presence in a child's life.

School has the potential to be an incredible support for children if it provides a safe, supportive environment with adults who are consistently present and compassionate. At the same time, we cannot take for granted that schools always provide only green boxes. School is sometimes a place where a child feels bullied, undermined, or less-than. Class can be a place where a child feels anxious, stressed, and unsuccessful. In fact, the school shutdowns and reopenings during COVID-19 revealed that some children found their stress and anxiety was alleviated when they were home. For others, school closures meant they were removed from their support system and they suffered. When a child in your class is exhibiting anxiety or depression, or when you learn about outside adversities, consider all the ways the child's school experience might be contributing red or green boxes to his or her scale.

Shifting the Fulcrum: Resilience-Promoting Skills

Shifting the fulcrum is one more fundamental way to make a child's scale tip toward a positive outcome—which is the core objective of this book. When we provide children with the kind of resilience-promoting skills that this book will explore in depth, we enable them to shift the fulcrum of their scale, making it easier for the positive supports to outweigh the negative experiences. As you improve a child's social, emotional, communication, and executive function skills, you build his or her internal resilience-promoting capacities. As an individual's fulcrum shifts, the red boxes are more easily offset by the green.

The Resilience Scale: Shifting the Fulcrum

NEGATIVE OUTCOME   POSITIVE OUTCOME

NEGATIVE EXPERIENCES

POSITIVE SUPPORTS

IMPROVE SKILLS AND ABILITIES

Notice that when the fulcrum shifts left (i.e., the child has increased his or her capacity for resilience), this helps offset the weight of the negative experiences.

The metaphor of the Resilience Scale illustrates how resilience works: External, environmental, and individual factors come together to offer the best chance to tip a child's scale toward positive lifelong outcomes.

It is important to understand that an individual's scale is not static. The red and green boxes change, and the fulcrum shifts over time and with educational and life experiences.

Communicating About Resilience

We find the Resilience Scale to be a powerful advocacy tool you can use to communicate with any stakeholder: a fellow educator, an administrator, a policymaker, a family member, or a student. The scale metaphor helps us frame resilience as being influenced by outside factors and fostered by internal capacities. This understanding shifts the burden of weathering adversity from the child to the community. It helps us avoid the damaging implication that some students can just bounce back naturally while others cannot. Framing resilience in this way can help stakeholders understand that they can contribute to a solution that supports the child.

When you think about and communicate about resilience, bear in mind not just what it is, but what it is not. The chart that follows helps clarify some common misconceptions.

What Resilience Is Not	What Resilience Is
Something you're born with	Resilience can be developed over time.
A fixed, unchanging trait	Resilience may evolve, grow, lessen, and fluctuate with different life circumstances.
An internal characteristic	Resilience is a set of skills and capacities that can be nurtured, learned, and developed.
An individual's responsibility	Providing supportive relationships and social supports is the responsibility of the caring adults in a child's world.
The ability to bounce back, like a rubber band	The ability to weather adversity through life's ups and downs, as with a scale
The absence of stress or adversity	The ability to adapt to stress and adversity that all people experience
The ability to cope on your own without help	The ability to seek and receive help from others
A one-time achievement	An ongoing process of growth and development
The ability to always be optimistic, no matter the circumstances	The ability to view a situation realistically and maintain a reasonably hopeful outlook

The Resilience Scale in Action

To think about the scale in real life, imagine this scenario: A new student has just walked into your third-grade classroom mid-November. You review her records, which reveal that she has attended two different poorly funded schools this academic year alone. The vice principal fills you in on a challenging situation at home: Her father recently lost his job, the only source of income for the family. The family has had to stay with different relatives until the financial situation stabilizes.

You might expect that this child would not do well in school and that she might show several maladaptive behaviors, including either being withdrawn or oppositional and disruptive. But you notice that she has some strengths and, even with all that is going on in her life, she responds well to you—she has some relationship-building skills in place. You see that she is curious, she wants to learn, she makes friends, and despite all that she is struggling with, she often thinks about others. One day you see her stop what she is doing to help a classmate struggling to understand a new project. Her resilience scale is clearly weighted toward positive outcomes. You ask yourself: How has this child sustained these important skills in the face of all the turbulence she has been facing? How can you help her continue to use and strengthen these skills? As you help her, can you do something for the other students in your room that would help them develop similar skills? Can teaching these skills be integrated into your already packed schedule?

When you look closely at a student's experiences and behaviors, consider how these would appear on the Resilience Scale.

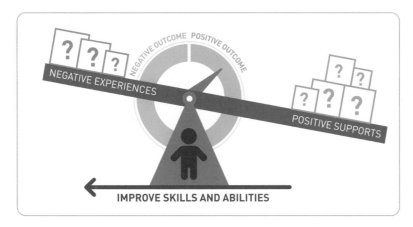

What are the child's red boxes? What are the known green boxes? Ask yourself questions such as the following:

- How can my classroom be a safe and supportive environment? (This gives all of the children in your classroom a "green box.")

- How can I become a crucial, supportive, and caring adult presence in this child's life?

- How can I help move this child's fulcrum by helping her to build resilience-promoting skills and capacities?

The Resilience Framework

We rely on a framework for thinking about resilience-promoting skills based on the ongoing research and experience of the Yale Child Study Center-Scholastic Collaborative for Child & Family Resilience. The Resilience Framework identifies the core capacities that support resilience and help move a child's fulcrum. The framework also offers specific skills and literacy strategies that help develop those capacities in children.

The framework is, in essence, a map of important resilience-promoting capacities to observe in your students and to provide practical ways to foster those skills as you go about your day-to-day teaching: (1) developing supportive relationships; (2) forming positive self-identities; (3) building curiosity and motivation; (4) engaging flexible thinking; and (5) demonstrating altruism.

Developing Strong Relationships	Forming Positive Self-Identities	Building Curiosity and Motivation	Engaging in Flexible Thinking	Demonstrating Altruism
Form strong connections with people who can support you.	Have a strong sense of who you are and develop confidence.	Be curious about the world around you and motivated to learn.	Welcome new information and ideas and think creatively.	Act for the benefit of your family, friends, and community.

To think about how these capacities come into play to foster resilience, let's focus on a particular child. Think of a student who has come to you facing many challenges, whom you've wanted desperately to help—one of the many children whom you recognize has potential and you think about even after the workday ends. Here, we'll talk about a child named Hendrix.

LOOKING AT RESILIENCE:
Hendrix's Story

Five-year-old Hendrix was moving with his family to a new city. As he prepared, he peppered his teacher at the school he was leaving with questions: Would he make new friends? What would school be like in the new location? Would his teacher be nice? Would he be able to eat his favorite foods? Was there a library there with his favorite book series? Was there a playground nearby?

His resilience-informed teacher understood that this move was a major stressor for Hendrix and tried to offer support. She thought about how she could help reinforce some of Hendrix's strengths in ways that would help him weather this change and thrive in his new town. She helped him write a list of all his questions and promised that together they would try to find out answers and record them in a journal. In this way, she supported his curiosity. She asked him to think about what he would like the new friends he would make to know about him. She helped him write an All About Me letter to share with new friends, which reinforced his sense of identity. She also asked his classmates to draw pictures and write notes for him to take with him. In this way, she helped the whole class develop empathy and altruism. She also told him that she was always going to remember him and would love to hear from him after he moved. In this way, she reinforced supportive relationships.

These are just a few examples of how a resilience-informed teacher can take intentional steps to tip a child's scale toward positive outcomes. Hendrix will surely have challenges with the move and may have a rocky adjustment. But he will enter that challenge with a few tools and the knowledge that his former teacher and classmates care for him and will miss him as he faces his new adventures ahead.

Resilience-Promoting Skills

The five capacities identified in the Resilience Framework can be fostered when children have the resilience-building skills shown in the table on the next page. The skills in the framework fall into four broad categories:

- Emotional Skills
- Social Skills
- Communication Skills
- Executive Function Skills

Take a moment to review the table of skill categories on page 27 and related behaviors you can look for as students interact with one another, with you, and with other school staff members. In which skill areas do your students demonstrate greater capacity? In which might they need more opportunities to develop?

For a more in-depth look at these skills, turn to the Resilience Framework on page 28. Notice how the specific skills in each category run across each of the resilience-building capacities. For example, consider the social skill of perspective-taking—the appreciation that you may have a different view or understanding of something

or someone because you've had a different experience. You use this skill every day. You might understand that a child is especially irritable because you know that his or her parent has been sick, while others may only see the child as displaying disruptive behaviors. You also use this skill when you read, understanding that a character has a different set of experiences and a different set of knowledge from you, the reader.

The chapters that follow highlight practical ways that you can nurture these skills in the classroom through the environment you create and the literacy instruction you design.

Skills Category	Definition	What to Look For
EMOTIONAL SKILLS	The ability to recognize, understand, and manage emotions effectively. This category includes building confidence, regulating emotions, and also recognizing the emotions of others.	Expressing feelings appropriately, identifying emotions in themselves and others, using coping strategies to manage their feelings, seeking help when needed
SOCIAL SKILLS	The ability to form positive relationships with others and to navigate social situations effectively	Engaging in cooperative play, showing compassion toward others, resolving conflicts peacefully and respectfully
COMMUNICATION SKILLS	The ability to express oneself clearly and effectively, and to listen and understand others	Engaging in group discussions, asking questions, and actively listening to others
EXECUTIVE FUNCTION SKILLS	The ability to set goals, make decisions, problem solve, and plan for the future. These skills help us make sense of the world and are foundational to taking wise action in our lives.	Setting goals, creating plans to achieve goals, breaking down tasks into manageable steps, managing time effectively, maintaining focus on tasks, persisting through challenges

The Resilience Framework

Resilience Capacities & Skills		Supportive Relationships	Self-Identity	Curiosity and Motivation	Flexible Thinking	Altruism
EMOTIONAL SKILLS	Building Self-Awareness and Confidence	●	●	●		
	Recognizing Emotions	●	●		●	
	Managing Emotions		●		●	●
	Empathizing	●	●			●
SOCIAL SKILLS	Respecting Others	●		●	●	●
	Working Collaboratively	●			●	●
	Asking for and Receiving Help	●	●		●	●
	Perspective-Taking	●		●	●	●
COMMUNICATION SKILLS	Communicating Effectively	●	●	●	●	●
	Active Listening	●	●	●	●	
	Storytelling	●	●	●	●	●
	Reframing	●		●	●	●
EXECUTIVE FUNCTION SKILLS	Making Decisions		●	●	●	
	Developing Persistence		●	●	●	
	Solving Problems	●		●	●	●
	Looking Forward		●	●	●	

Using Literacy to Build Resilience

We believe it's most effective to incorporate the resilience-promoting skills into the instruction and activities that are already happening throughout your school day.

For example, you can use math instruction to foster persistence and problem-solving. History can be a great vehicle for building empathy and perspective-taking. In science class, forming a hypothesis, testing, evaluating, and drawing conclusions are all connected to executive function.

But for us, literacy instruction is the most extraordinary vehicle for developing resilience-promoting skills. On a fundamental level, narrative and storytelling are essential to the human condition (Green et al., 2006). Having a sense of origin, of beginning, middle, and end, helps define where we come from, who we are, and where we are going. On a developmental level, literacy can help children develop self-awareness, emotional skills, and empathy. Reading about the lives of characters

Kids Demonstrating Resilience: The I Survived Series

Few children's book series provide clearer examples of resilience among young people than author Lauren Tarshis's popular **I Survived** series. These stories from history, some in graphic novel form and many available in Spanish, feature young characters whose resilience gets them through some of the most memorable and terrifying events in history, including the destruction of Pompeii in 79 CE, the Great Chicago Fire of 1871, the 1912 sinking of the Titanic, the Hindenburg disaster in 1937, the 1967 attack of the Grizzlies, the 1980 eruption of Mount St. Helens, and many more. Check the Scholastic website to read more about these books and how the young people featured in them demonstrated the skills needed to survive such challenging experiences.

broadens a child's understanding of himself or herself and others; story plots develop critical-thinking skills and can model problem-solving and persistence. Talking about what they are reading provides a safe way for children to explore their own feelings and to discuss their own experiences.

The Resilience Framework places a special emphasis on using storytelling and narrative to develop the different resilience-promoting skills. From journaling to creative writing to discussion groups, we know that providing children opportunities to tell their stories and express their unique perspectives is key to supporting them through challenging times. To this end, we include a few ideas here for getting started with storytelling.

Weaving Storytelling Into Your Day

Create a storytelling routine: Set aside a designated time for children to share their stories about what has happened during their day. This could be during circle time or morning meeting or at the close of the day. The goal is to honor their stories with few to no interruptions.

Incorporate digital storytelling: Encourage students to bring their stories to life using digital tools. Consider using digital story platforms that allow children to plot stories, animate, narrate, and add soundtracks to create digital stories.

Write what matters most: Give children regular opportunities to write about or draw what matters to them. When children have time each week to consistently and freely write about topics they care about, they develop the habit of expressing themselves more clearly. This writing should not be evaluated. Set aside time for children to share their stories with their classmates if they like. Children can offer feedback to one another when requested, with guidance on how to give specific and helpful responses. Here are a few prompts:

- One thing that you did well...
- I learned this from your writing...
- The part that I find fascinating is...

Encourage Family Storytelling

Families are steeped in the rich stories and oral traditions that are an integral part of many cultures, particularly in Black and Brown communities. Dinner time or other family time can be optimal for families to share the oral traditions of who they are. Think of different ways you can encourage family storytelling. You may want to:

- Send home prompts that encourage family discussions about topics students have been talking or writing about in school.
- Ask families to make digital recordings of family stories that they would like to share with the class.
- Invite families to send in artifacts that are important to their family and have children talk about these artifacts with their classmates.

With permission, you may want to put together a collection of family stories that can be enjoyed by other classrooms.

Summary of Key Points

- An individual's capacity for resilience in the face of challenge is determined both by environmental factors and the skills he or she has acquired to manage his or her response to challenges—this dynamic is described with a Resilience Scale model.
- Using this model as a frame, educators and caregivers have the opportunity to 1) create environments that add more positive factors (green boxes) to the positive outcome side of the scale; and 2) help children develop skills that shift the fulcrum to help offset negative experiences.
- The Resilience Framework features five resilience-promoting capacities that educators and other adults can help students actively develop. When the capacity for resilience grows, we can shift the fulcrum of the Resilience Scale in a way that helps us achieve positive outcomes.

The chapters that follow explore each of the resilience-promoting capacities in detail. Our hope is that as you apply the Resilience Framework to your daily practice and learn how to help children move the fulcrum on the Resilience Scale, you will be better able to answer the Maasai greeting, *Kasserian Ingera*? or "How are the children?" with "The children are well and we did what was needed."

CHAPTER 2

DEVELOPING SUPPORTIVE RELATIONSHIPS

"I have come to believe that in order to thrive, a child must have at least one adult in her life who shows her unconditional love, respect, and confidence."

—Sonia Sotomayor

Take a moment to make a list of all the people with whom you have supportive, positive relationships. Put a check mark beside those on your list that you consider trustworthy confidantes. These are the people you can likely be vulnerable with without the fear of shame and ridicule. Now circle the names of those you know with all certainty you can depend on when circumstances in your life become difficult and hard to manage. These are the people who will be by your side doing everything possible to support you mentally, emotionally, socially, and financially, if necessary—the people who "have your back" at all costs. Now ask the following questions:

- What characteristics do these people possess that let you know they are dependable?

- What actions have they taken to reassure you they are in your corner, no matter what?

- If someone else were making this list, would your name show up with a check mark?

- What makes you the person that others can depend on?

When we consider how critical relationships are in our lives, it's no surprise that the American Psychological Association emphasizes that one of the primary factors for resilience is having caring, supportive relationships—with those we call our family (biological or not) and our closest friends (Holt-Lunstad, Robles, & Sbarra, 2017). This chapter explores how children's resilience can be developed through the relationships you build and promote in your classroom community.

As Humans, We Need Social Connections

Humans are gregarious. We thrive on a range of social connections, from the people we share laughs with to the most trusted people whose names are checked on our lists above. Our social relationships sustain us and are essential for our well-being, preventing loneliness and isolation, and promoting health benefits such as longevity, less depression, and less stress, just to name a few. And there's more from a resilience perspective: Studies document that people who have the support of family, friends, and community members are happier, have an improved sense of self-worth, and have a stronger sense of belonging. They are also better able to weather the stresses of life (Umberson & Montez, 2010). Our understanding of the impact of social connections was heightened during COVID-19 when those who had strong social networks tended to fare better (Nitschke, et al., 2021).

Strong social relationships are essential for children. Relationships are a vitally important part of a child's identity development. When a child has a sense of belonging, the child learns (and believes) that he or she matters and is a part of something bigger than himself or herself. Children seek out friendships for approval, decision-making, social support, and a sense of belonging at school. We want to help our students develop strong, healthy peer relationships that benefit everyone

A Culturally Responsive Foundation for Building Supportive Relationships

In *Revolutionary Love: Creating a Culturally Inclusive Literacy Classroom* (2022), Michele and her colleagues show how becoming aware of our own culturally informed social identities and biases, challenging our beliefs, and changing our behaviors toward our students, enables us to support their cultural, racial, or linguistic identities (Wynter-Hoyte et al., 2022). When we affirm our students, we lay the groundwork for healthy teacher-student and peer relationships. And, as we'll explore in more depth in Chapter 3, teaching in a culturally responsive way recognizes the tremendous assets and strengths our students bring into our classrooms, which is essential to their developing strong self-identities— a second resilience capacity.

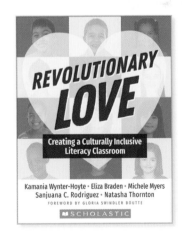

involved, including teachers. The more students develop better relationship skills, the more likely they are to be self-assured and contribute to a positive classroom culture.

As teachers, we also want to develop strong, supportive relationships with our students. While it can be difficult to make an individual, personal connection with each student, our caring presence and actions can positively impact every one—particularly those who need a trustworthy adult who the student feels has his or her back.

In light of your role in your students' support network, consider the exercise at the beginning of this chapter. For some children, you may be one of the few or even the only positive relationship they can depend on, so showing each child that he or she matters to you will build trust, a key to ensuring a safe emotional space for risk-taking and learning. Even those students who have an extensive network of positive relationships at home and school will benefit from your efforts at forming supportive relationships across the roster; you both reinforce their social network and model how a dependable, caring person behaves. They, in turn, can practice the same behaviors with their peers.

Shifting the Fulcrum Through Positive Connections

Students from all backgrounds and ages benefit from supportive, positive relationships (Sethi & Scales, 2020), and students with the greatest academic and behavioral challenges may benefit the most (DuBois et al., 2011). When a child has a strong web of relationships that includes family members, teachers, friends, mentors, coaches, neighbors, and more, the child will more likely flourish and develop the skills necessary to deal with adversities in life (Roehlkepartain et al., 2017; Sippel et al., 2015). Children will know that they are not alone with their difficulties and will be able to draw on the collective strength of those in their networks to sustain and bolster their own strength.

Relationships that foster trust and growth can strengthen children's resilience-building capacities (Hartling, 2008). Once trust is established in a relationship, children learn that they can count on the individual and the connection becomes stronger. The more positive, trusting relationships a child has, the more a child's fulcrum shifts so that his or her scale more easily tips toward the positive even when there are negative conditions on the other side. This is important to consider in light of the recent COVID-19 pandemic and forced social distancing, which caused many students to experience higher levels of isolation and loneliness that contributed to an increase in depression and anxiety. We believe that only in time will we fully grasp the extent to which all of us, and especially children, have been impacted by the pandemic. But as members of our students' networks, we can be proactive in helping them deal with possible psychological stresses and equip them with skills to shift their fulcrum in an optimal direction.

Relationships that foster trust and growth can strengthen children's resilience-building capacities.

In the story that follows, we share how Ms. Martin, a supportive teacher in Ollie's network, rallied his classmates and others in the school and community to help Ollie overcome several obstacles that life presented him and his family.

THE IMPORTANCE OF RELATIONSHIPS:
Ollie's Story

Shortly after the pandemic lockdown ended, Ollie eagerly joined his classmates back in school. Those first days back were a big adjustment for everyone and Ollie's teacher, Ms. Martin, did her best to help bring the class back together. But in time, she noticed that Ollie's attendance had become sporadic. Ms. Martin could see that the absences were taking a toll. Ollie was a bright student who loved to learn, but when he was able to come to class, he often drifted off and stared into space rather than participating. When Ms. Martin tried to include him, he would look at the floor in response. Then, just as he would seem to start to catch on, he would miss school again.

Ms. Martin decided to investigate. After talking to his family, the school nurse, and front office staff, Ms. Martin learned about the challenges that Ollie and his family were facing. Ollie's family struggled financially; they lived in a house without heat or reliable transportation to the bus stop. Ollie didn't have a warm winter coat.

With the help of the school nurse, principal, and Ollie's family, Ms. Martin brought together neighborhood and community resources. She let Ollie know that she and the class missed him when he was out of school and that they wanted to make sure Ollie felt like the important member of the class that he was—and to see him succeed as he did when he could learn with them every day. They wanted to make sure he didn't miss any more school. The team reached out to a concerned neighbor who lived near Ollie's family; the neighbor offered to give him a ride to the bus stop every day. The principal organized a drive for coats and other supplies, not just for Ollie's family, but for anyone in the school community who needed them. Ollie's classmates helped him catch up from missed class time, and Ms. Martin made sure Ollie worked closely with a partner during daily small-group time. Soon, Ollie was back to participating fully in class, his love of learning intact. He answered questions, collaborated with classmates, and focused on his work. No more drifting off and staring at the floor.

Thanks to the combined efforts of Ms. Martin, Ollie's classmates, neighbors, and the school community, Ollie was able to receive new, warm clothing, a backpack with school supplies, and help with transportation. But most important, Ollie saw that he had a number of people in his life who cared.

Connecting Ollie's Story to Resilience-Promoting Skills

A child's first supportive relationships are formed with the adults who care for him or her. Having strong, positive relationships with one's caregivers gives a child a sense of security that enables him or her to venture out into the world with the confidence to participate. When we teachers take notice of the children in our class and pick up on behavioral clues, we show that we care. We show them that we have their backs. Ollie's reluctance to participate signaled to Ms. Martin that something was wrong. Ollie's absences were making it hard for him not only to learn and participate but also to form meaningful relationships with his teacher and classmates. Ms. Martin sought help resolving the practical problems, like ensuring Ollie's transportation to school, while she also helped to create a caring and inclusive environment for every student, including Ollie. In doing so, she was able to help Ollie build self-confidence. He could see that he mattered to his teacher and classmates, and that his participation and contributions were essential. With a trusting, caring class environment, Ollie was developing his skills in working collaboratively and communicating effectively. As he was integrated back into the classroom, Ollie was learning what it means to be an integral part of a classroom community.

Tipping the Scale for Ollie: Supportive Relationships

Positive, supportive relationships are always important but they become even more so during distressing times. For many students like Ollie and his classmates, the pandemic had reverberations that lasted beyond the actual lockdown. Add to this a family's financial difficulties and we see a lot of red boxes stacking up on the negative side of a child's scale. Ms. Martin took action to make sure that the hardships Ollie faced were counterbalanced by strong, supportive relationships he could rely on. The collaborative efforts of the support team she brought together gave Ollie the opportunity to experience the benefits of having supportive relationships—he was able to continue learning and participating as a valued member of his class. In this way, Ollie's fulcrum nudged toward the positive side of the scale, shifting the balance, and introducing Ollie to an essential life skill—being able to look to and rely on help from others in the face of hardship. Notably, Ollie was not the only one in a position to learn and grow from this experience: The entire school-community team who rallied their support for Ollie gained the opportunity to expand their own resilience capacities by taking altruistic action, which we'll learn more about in Chapter 6.

When the Scale Tips in the Negative Direction

We shared the importance of positive student-adult relationships. When we don't see our students as individuals with needs, wants, and desires, we miss the opportunities to truly connect with them and form lasting relationships. In addition, psychological stress can impact a child's willingness to build strong relationships with others and can often be exhibited in a child's behavior.

We want children to understand that true friends accept them for who they are and challenge them to become better.

According to the National Institute of Mental Health, the following behaviors may indicate that a child is dealing with psychological stresses (NIMH, 2021):

- the inability to sit quietly; increased irritability

- having excessive fears and worries

- problems with sleeplessness

- frequent stomachaches or headaches without a clear cause

Social relationships matter because they help our children manage feelings of anxiety, stress, and other difficult emotions. The presence of strong relationships also helps children respond when challenging situations present themselves.

Because children tend to emulate others in their social circles, it is important for children to surround themselves with peers who have positive dispositions. In this way, they can authentically be themselves without fear of ridicule. We want children to understand that true friends accept them for who they are and challenge them to become better. When children feel the need to put on pretenses, their true selves are hidden behind the many facades that they must perform to fit in. It's hard for them to make meaningful connections when they are hiding their true selves. Even more troubling is when a child is alienated from social groups, bullied, and isolated, which can lead to depression and other negative outcomes. We can assist our students by being attuned to their emotional needs, which is essential in helping them learn coping skills.

Helping Families Encourage Strong Relationships

You can encourage families to support their children in forming strong relationships through literature. Family Book Clubs offer children opportunities to read and engage in critical discussions of texts (Wynter-Hoyte et al., 2022) with caring members of their families. These discussions will extend a child's understanding of the texts beyond the words written on the pages. These discussions may even present opportunities for children and family members to develop deeper bonds based on their shared interests. Families may need your assistance in finding high quality, anti-biased literature. The Teaching for Change site offers an Anti-Bias Education page with book lists and other great resources that you can share with families.

Strong Relationships in Our Literacy Classrooms and Beyond

Is there a student in your classroom who typically struggles with peer social interaction? Do you have that kid who just doesn't seem to fit in? Are you aware of a child who is experiencing bullying at the hands of his or her classmates? Do you have a student who may be a bit depressed? The skills and strategies we provide below will not replace counseling if that is what a child needs (and if you feel that a child does need psychological assistance, we urge you to help coordinate that).

What we do offer below are some general routines and strategies that you can do as professionals to teach children the skills they need to make healthy relationships and connect positively with you and their classmates.

Look to literature for models of positive social relationships. High-quality children's books often show children how to build supportive relationships by being a good friend and working through the ups and downs of friendships. Books can serve as the springboard for discussions about character relationships with the whole group, in a small group, or one-on-one. Helpful formats include Socratic Seminars and Literature Circles.

Extend your literature study by weaving it into your writing time. You might have children write responses to the text, letters to the characters, or different endings to the stories. As a reminder, it is important to select books that bring joy (Muhammad, 2023), prompt curiosity, and provide solace,

Socratic Seminars and Literature Circles

Socratic Seminars is a teaching strategy based on Socrates's belief in developing students' abilities to critically analyze a topic as they dialogue with others. To begin, students read a common text. They are then divided into two circles—an inner circle and outer circle. The inner circle discusses the text first while the outer circle listens, takes notes, and notices patterns in responses. Then the roles switch (Copeland, 2005). In this way, students get to discuss meaningful elements like character interactions in a smaller group, while also listening and observing how their peers interact—a double dose of learning about navigating social relationships.

Literature Circles engage a small group of students in a series of student-led meetings to discuss a book, much like a book club (Daniels, 2002). Sometimes students take different roles during the discussions; for instance, as Awesome Illustrator, Word Wizard, Discussion Director, Connector, and so on.

as well as books that serve as windows, mirrors, and sliding glass doors (Bishop, 1990) where children find themselves and their stories reflected in the pages. What follows are a few titles we suggest that speak to the importance of supportive relationships.

Grades K–2

I Am Enough **by Grace Byers** Grace Byers's picture book is a heartfelt ode to self-love and compassion, inviting readers on a journey of embracing individuality and celebrating our differences. With Keturah A. Bobo's vibrant illustrations, girls of diverse bodies, cultures, and abilities come to life. The book empowers readers to see the importance of diversity and cultivating relationships with those who celebrate and uplift us.

A Thousand White Butterflies **by Jessica Betancourt-Perez and Karen Lynn Williams** Inspired by the lives of authors Jessica Betancourt-Perez and Karen Lynn Williams, this picture book follows Isabella—a young girl who has just moved to the United States from Colombia. When Isabella's first day of school is canceled due to heavy snowfall, she finds herself missing her warm home country and worrying that she'll never make new friends. Through Gina Maldonado's adorable illustrations, readers discover that friendships can blossom even in the most snowy and unfamiliar places.

When a Friend Needs a Friend **by Roozeboos** Best friends Aya and Oskar love to envision and build extraordinary creations together, especially at the construction site where Oskar's uncle works. When Oskar suddenly begins to feel sad and withdrawn, Aya is not sure how to help. Roozeboos's picture book focuses on these deep

emotions and teaches young readers how to support their friends as they navigate overwhelming feelings.

Grades 3–5

***Falling Short* by Ernesto Cisneros** Ernesto Cisneros's uplifting novel follows two young Latino boys who, despite being best friends, are incredibly different. Isaac is a gifted athlete struggling to keep up with his academic work, while what Marco lacks in athleticism he makes up for with his excellent grades. As the boys prepare for a life-changing year in sixth grade, they help each other strive to gain approval from their respective fathers. As Isaac and Marco navigate these pressures, they form an unbreakable bond and offer each other the approval they're desperately searching for.

***Number the Stars* by Lois Lowry** When the German troops begin their forced relocation of Jews in Denmark during World War II, Annemarie's family rushes to take in her best friend, Ellen Rosen, and pass her off as part of their family. In Lois Lowry's poignant novel, readers discover the remarkable bond of the two friends and the notion of power in numbers while also learning about the heroic efforts of the Danish Resistance to lead nearly their entire Jewish population to safety in Sweden.

***Strange Birds: A Field Guide to Ruffling Feathers* by Celia C. Pérez** In a quiet Florida town, a group of young girls make a shocking discovery—a local scout troop has been illegally gathering bird feathers for their ceremonial hats. Outraged, the girls form their own troop, navigating a series of challenges in their quest to ignite social change and reveal the truth. Celia C. Pérez's novel explores the compelling themes of friendship, community, and the power of sisterhood.

Summary of Key Points

- As humans, we are social. We need each other. Relationships that foster trust and growth can strengthen children's resilience-building capacities.

- Children need supportive, trusting relationships as they forge their way through this world. A teacher is sometimes one of the few trusting adults that a child can depend on.

- Oftentimes, our students with the greatest academic and behavioral challenges are the ones who need our support the most.

- Supportive relationships can lessen a child's physiological and psychological stresses.

In the pages that follow are some classroom-tested routines and activities to help you foster the kinds of supportive relationships that your students may need. Many of these activities and routines address the four skill groups we identified in the previous chapter: emotional skills, social skills, communication skills, and executive function skills.

ROUTINES AND ACTIVITIES FOR DEVELOPING SUPPORTIVE RELATIONSHIPS

	Routines and Activities	Social Skill	Emotional Skill	Communication Skill	Executive Function Skill	Page Number
ROUTINES	Learn Students' Names	●	●	●		47
ROUTINES	Spend One-on-One Time With Students	●	●	●		47
ROUTINES	Attend Their Events	●	●	●		47
ACTIVITIES	Just Like Me Game	●	●	●	●	48
ACTIVITIES	Whose Bucket Do You Fill?	●	●	●	●	50
ACTIVITIES	Classmates Pact	●	●	●	●	52
ACTIVITIES	You Are Appreciated	●	●	●	●	54

Learn Students' Names

Becoming your students' most trusted adult in school starts with honoring their names; In *Life, Literacy, and the Pursuit of Happiness*, former principal Don Vu encourages us to avoid calling children by names other than the given names they come to us with for ease of pronunciation or to help the child "fit in." When a teacher does this, he or she is sending the message to the child that his or her identity is problematic (2020). One of the best ways you can build positive relationships with and among your students is to learn their names as quickly as possible, pronounce them correctly, and use them in positive ways. Ask the child which name he or she prefers you and the other students use. Then ask (and ensure) that classmates use that name when referring to that student. You may consider adding books about names to your classroom library. Reading Juana Martinez-Neal's *Alma and How She Got Her Name* may help students understand that all names are special.

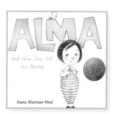

Spend One-on-One Time With Students

You may be wondering where you might fit one-on-one conversations into your schedule. Consider breaks and transitions. You can spend 5–10 minutes talking with a selected child during recess, lunch, or before or after school. During these one-on-one moments, set your focus on getting to know the child beyond just academics. Ask children about themselves, their families, things they like to do, and places they like to go. Sharing in turn about yourself helps your students see you as a person and not just their teacher. You can speak about your pets, your hobbies, books you enjoy, or something new you just learned.

Attend Their Events

One of the best ways to build relationships with your students is to attend their events, when possible. There is nothing like the expression on a child's face when the child looks in the audience or in the stands and sees his or her teacher cheering him or her on. The smile that radiates from deep within affirms that the child knows that he or she matters to you. Attending students' events will also give you more information about the child to build on in your relationship—and in your teaching.

Just Like Me Game

Finding things we have in common with others, such as a shared hobby or similar experience, can help us forge friendships. Great for bonding early in the year, this sharing and comparing activity encourages active listening and empathic responses, which help students to deepen connections with their classmates.

FORMAT: Small or whole group

1. **Start with students seated in a circle.** Invite them to think of a few fun facts that their peers might not know about them. Designate one student as the leader. Have the leader stand and share a fun fact about an interest or hobby ("I like learning about constellations"), family or friends ("I have three brothers"), or an experience ("I went camping this summer").

2. **Everyone to whom the fun fact applies then stands up and says, "Just like me!"** Invite one or two of the standing students to share a detail about their similar interest or experience but keep the sharing brief to keep the game moving.

3. **For each round, have the previous leader choose the next leader to share a fun fact, interest, or experience.** If students have a lot to share, consider doing the activity over two sessions to make sure everyone has a chance to share. You might extend the activity by encouraging students to connect with a peer they found a shared interest with.

TIPS

FOR GRADES K–2: Model the activity for a younger group of students, showing how a leader shares a fun fact and how the rest of the class will either sit or stand in response. As students participate, provide guiding prompts to help them share specific details about what they have in common with their peer(s). For example, "Do you also have three dogs?"; "Tell us why he is just like you!"; and "Wow! That's something you all have in common with each other!"

FOR GRADES 3–5: You may choose to place students in pairs so they can get to know each other in a more focused way by investigating what they have in common. Ask each partner to share five to 10 fun facts. Then the pair can jot down all the commonalities they've discovered together. Guide them as they work on developing their list, reminding them to think about cultural background, goals, or passions as commonalities. Then invite them to share their list to the class in pairs. Students can show a thumbs-up when they hear something they also share in common with the pair.

Fun Facts About Me

My grandparents come from Japan.

I'm in choir.

I want to be an aerospace engineer.

I like playing basketball.

My favorite food is pizza.

Whose Bucket Do You Fill?

This activity is an excellent way for students to work on building a close-knit classroom community by extending kindness to their peers and recognizing the ways kindness has been shown back to them. Students will work toward achieving the goal of being bucket fillers—people who are self-aware and compassionate toward others—and learn how these actions can strengthen relationships in their personal and educational environments.

FORMAT: Small or whole group

1. **Introduce the idea of bucket fillers versus bucket dippers—people who use words and actions that negatively impact others.** Draw two buckets on a whiteboard or posterboard labeled *Bucket Fillers* and *Bucket Dippers* to help students visualize the activity.

2. **Model the activity by sharing an example of an action from both a bucket filler or dipper.** If you say, "sticking up for a classmate," think aloud as you assign the action to the bucket labeled *Bucket Filler*.

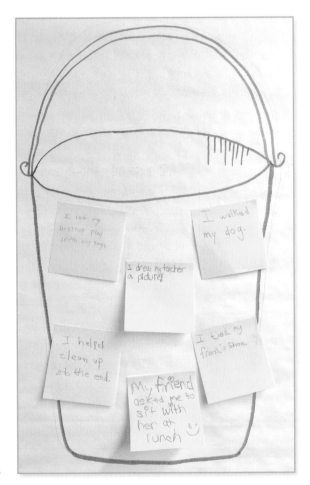

Students' Bucket Filler notes

3. **Provide students with two self-stick notes, asking them to jot down one act of kindness they've shown to their peers and one act of kindness that has been shown to them.** Circulate and confer with students as they work.

4. **Invite students to place their self-stick notes on the bucket labeled *Bucket Filler*.** Read some of the notes aloud as you guide students to think about the ways being a bucket filler helps create a loving and safe classroom community.

5. **Once complete, invite the whole group to share how they will focus on being a bucket filler for the week to come.** You may write these ideas down on a large notepad or chart paper to set your goals for a "Week of Kindness." Have the class return to the goals at the end of the week and share the acts of kindness they performed or witnessed.

TIPS

FOR GRADES K–2: You can adapt this goal-setting activity for a younger group by asking students to choose a single bucket-filler action and having them perform that action during the week of kindness. Have students share their acts of kindness at the end of the week as you provide guiding questions that help them understand the importance of the action they displayed.

FOR GRADES 3–5: For an older group of students, you may choose to extend the activity by asking students to write a short essay about the acts of kindness they performed or witnessed and how they will continue being bucket fillers.

Classroom Pact

A safe and inviting classroom environment is all the more meaningful when students take part in creating it. This activity enables students to work together on a classroom pact to outline specific behaviors that help cultivate supportive relationships, inclusion, and mutual respect. Students can reference their pact throughout the year to encourage them and hold them accountable in their work to implement these relationship-building behaviors in the classroom community.

FORMAT: Whole group

1. **Have students brainstorm ways they can help build supportive relationships with their classmates and make sure everyone is welcome and included.**

2. **After students have shared their ideas, introduce the activity and define the purpose of a pact.** Explain how a classroom pact will help guide students toward implementing those important steps they brainstormed, and how referencing the pact will hold them accountable for their progress.

3. **Invite each student to write an idea on the same piece of poster or chart paper.** You may also wish to contribute an idea. Ask students to add decorations if they like.

4. **Display the classroom pact in a prominent place so that students can refer to it throughout the year.**

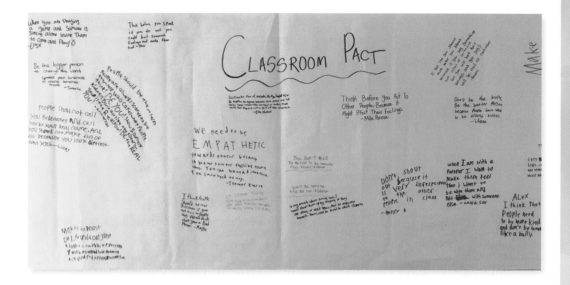

TIPS

FOR GRADES K–2: Take the lead in the brainstorming session. Encourage active listening while the brainstorming session is happening—you can mention how allowing space to be heard helps create a supportive classroom community with peers who trust and respect each other. Once each student has verbally contributed an idea for the pact, have them write or illustrate that idea on a self-stick note and stick it onto the larger poster board.

FOR GRADES 3–5: For an older elementary group, you may decide to include an additional step when inviting students to contribute their written ideas onto the poster board. After students have added their ideas, ask them to explain why they chose to include that statement or goal in the pact. It may be helpful to provide guiding questions, such as, "You said you chose to write 'make sure everyone gets a turn in class,' because you think it's a nice thing to do. How can it make people feel when they don't get a turn?"

You Are Appreciated

By asking children to think about a teacher or staff member who is special to them, they can begin to identify the adults who make up their support network at school. This activity enables students to communicate appreciation and express gratitude through a written letter to their favorite teacher or staff member. An appreciation letter can help deepen a student's bond with a significant adult in his or her life and can provide you with tools to evaluate how to best build trust with each student depending on his or her unique needs.

FORMAT: Small or whole group

1. **Ask students to think about a favorite teacher or staff member, encouraging them to consider ways the adult made them feel supported, confident, or capable.** Have them also think of ways the teacher or staff member has aided in their growth, which may include helping them learn a new skill, take risks, and try new things.

2. **Invite students to use the ideas above to draft a letter to their favorite teacher.** Circulate and offer guidance.

3. **Have students peer-edit their letter with a partner.** This will provide a space to share ideas, bond over their favorite teachers, and ensure a polished draft for delivery.

4. **Invite students to share their letters with their favorite teacher.** You may choose to hang copies of the letters in the hallways or entryways to create a "wall of appreciation" for the school community.

> **YOU ARE APPRECIATED!**
>
> Dear Mrs. Tanaka,
> I'm writing this letter because you're my favorite teacher. I was shy when school started, but you changed everything.
> You always make me feel like I can do anything. You teach us cool things I love it when you read to us. You showed us how to be good classmates and work in teams. You make me love coming to school.
>
> Yours Truly,
> Devan

TIPS

FOR GRADES K–2: When asking students to share ways their favorite teacher has impacted them, it may be helpful to provide guiding questions to help them consider why this teacher is special to them. For a younger elementary group, you may invite students to also draw pictures or decorate their list/letter to best represent the way they feel about their favorite teacher.

FOR GRADES 3–5: You may choose to extend this activity by hosting a "letter-writing workshop," complete with stationery and envelopes. This extension can help students practice writing letters and sending them in the mail. In turn, they can begin to understand the importance that different modes of communication play in building and maintaining relationships. Place a template on the board to guide students in addressing their envelopes properly. If their teacher is at the same school, you may wish to take a trip as a class to place the envelopes in the teacher's mailbox. If not, you can invite students to scan and send the letters by email.

CHAPTER 3

FORMING POSITIVE SELF-IDENTITIES

> *"You'll never decide what you want until you've decided who you are."*
>
> —Noël Coward

How would you describe yourself to someone who doesn't know you? How would your closest friend or family member describe you? How would a colleague describe you? These questions probe your identity. The first one asks how you understand yourself, and the second and third ones ask how you present yourself to the world. For children developing resilience-promoting skills, the answers to those questions will help them gain a sense of self, develop confidence in navigating the world, and build supportive relationships with others.

Our self-identity is formed from the stories we hear as well as our personal experiences.

From the moment they are born, children are exposed to information that teaches them who they are. Parents and older siblings tell them stories about themselves as babies. They may hear stories about how they are "just like" their mother, father, uncle, or aunt, or they may be told about the dreams their families have for them when they grow up. Our self-identity is formed from the stories we hear as well as our personal experiences. We write and rewrite our "self-story" throughout our lives.

Typically, small children begin with a strong sense of self. Think about how often three-year-olds declare adamantly what they do or do not want and that they can do something all by themselves. Unfortunately, even early on, this strong sense of self can be eroded when the child feels unseen, unsupported, or criticized by the important people in the child's life or by negative subtle messages received from society about his or her self-worth. This results in children showing up in the world less confident and trying to adapt to who the world wants them to be. Even as adults, sometimes it is difficult to authentically show up in the world with all our vulnerabilities. Showing up authentically in the world requires trust and courage. At the same time, there will always be some differences between our private and public selves. We need to have some space between our private and public selves to help us adapt to the demands of our social and work worlds. But generally, the more aligned our private and public identities are, the freer and happier we feel. We feel more authentic, and others see us as authentic.

Self-Identity and Our Social Worlds

Self-identity is your internal awareness of who you are. Identity development is a complex, multifaceted, ongoing process and is influenced by many factors, including your interactions with the important people in your lives and whether you feel you fit into the many social environments in which you participate. Self-identity separates you from, as well as connects you to, others. Your sense of self and how you perceive your identity influence how you view your successes, your failures, your relationships, your values, and your overall purpose in life. The sociocultural groups you belong to may either support or challenge your sense of self, especially if identifying with a group conflicts with a perceived norm. Take, for instance, people who identify as transgender in a world that only acknowledges gender binaries. It may be hard for those people to authentically show up in the world as their true selves. They may feel the need to present themselves as people they truly are not, just to fit in with societal expectations. When children are uncomfortable in their own skin in important places such as school and at home, this may cause friction that threatens their social, emotional, and academic growth. Think about a time when you felt extremely comfortable just being you. What made it possible for you to be comfortable in your own skin with no pretenses?

- Was it because you were surrounded by caring individuals who saw, understood, and valued you?

- Was it because the social environment was familiar and welcoming? Was it your inner confidence in yourself?

- Or was it a combination of all these things?

Now think about a time when you felt extremely uncomfortable just being you. What changed?

Shifting the Fulcrum Through Positive Self-Identity

Having a strong, positive self-identity is one of the capacities that is foundational for building resilience-promoting skills. When children are secure in who they are, they are more likely to feel confident in a variety of social settings and are more capable of handling the negative factors in life and learning lessons from those negative factors to apply in the future. Helping a child develop a positive self-identity is one of the ways that you help the child shift his or her fulcrum toward positive outcomes. Developing a positive identity at an early age is important because it correlates with self-esteem, competence, and perseverance—and it promotes a sense of belonging. When a child has a strong, positive self-identity, the child feels loved, valued, and worthy (Keshky & Samak, 2017; Dweck, 2017) and the child knows who he or she is and what he or she values about himself or herself. A child who is forming a strong, positive self-identity may exhibit some of the following characteristics:

- optimistic

- tends to perform well in school

- open to diverse points of view and differences among his or her peers

- doesn't feel the need to put others down to feel better about himself or herself

- proud of who he or she is and what he or she accomplishes

- comfortable asking for help

- recognizes his or her potential and strengths as an individual

When you think of the characteristics listed above, which students in your class come to mind? What behaviors are they exhibiting that show this capacity in development? Who are the students who may not be developing these characteristics? What concerns you about them? What can you do to assist?

Sometimes, when young children start school, they may assume that their classmates' experiences, culture, and linguistic practices are similar to their own.

Then they become aware that each family and home has cultural and linguistic ways of being that are different. Following this may be a period of evaluation, judgment, and potential self-doubt. This recognition of differences is an important time for reinforcing the idea that differences are a source of strength and not of deficiency, both in children's own lives and in the lives of others. We invite you to meet Ms. Amy Britt, a resilience-informed teacher, who makes intentional decisions to cultivate a learning environment where differences are viewed as assets and not deficits. In doing so, we share a story about Luna, one of the students in Ms. Britt's room.

APPRECIATING DIFFERENCES:
Luna's Story

One afternoon, Luna joined her after-school tutoring group for a special activity. Ms. Britt asked each child in the group to bring a picture of something or someone important to her or him. When the children arrived, they saw that Ms. Britt had laid out on the floor a map that she'd traced of their small community. "Put your picture where you live," Ms. Britt instructed. At first, Luna stood by while her classmates sprang into action. As they tumbled over each other to place their pictures, bits of stories also tumbled out—a cousin, a trip to the local park, a birthday, a visit with grandmother, and so on.

Of all the children, Luna was the most tentative. She was extremely shy and quiet. She was also the only student in the class whose home language was Spanish. Though Luna spoke and read English well, she seemed hesitant, even afraid, to try to read aloud. She rarely took risks and did not socialize with her peers.

That afternoon, with some help from Ms. Britt, Luna found a long road on the map and said that her *abuelita* lived off that road. She traced the road with her finger and quietly put a picture of a black and white dog just off the road. One of her classmates came over to look at her picture and asked, "Is that your dog?" Luna nodded. Another child asked about the dog's name. "Dulce," she whispered. Ms. Britt wondered if there was more that Luna might share about Dulce. In a

Continued from previous page

soft voice, Luna said that she and Dulce played together every day after school, and he came to her room at night. "Sounds like Dulce is a good friend," Ms. Britt replied. Luna nodded but continued to sit quietly and watch. Addressing the group, Ms. Britt commented that everyone has stories to tell about their pictures, "When you tell a story, you are making a connection with someone else. This is how we learn about each other."

Luna stood up and walked around the paper to look at the other pictures. She told Ms. Britt that she and Dulce liked to run as fast as they could up and down the gravel road to their house and that her *abuelita* sometimes gave Dulce special treats when she was cooking. Other students started to ask more questions—where did she get Dulce, what did the word *dulce* mean, was Dulce still a pup, could he chase rabbits, could he swim, did she brush him? Luna seemed both to relax and get the idea that it was safe to talk more— and others would listen. She was discovering that she could share important words about her life that she knew were unfamiliar to the other students like *abuelita* and *dulce* and they could find connections to their lives.

Soon it was time for parents, grandparents, and others to come pick up the children from school. When Luna's *abuelita* came to get her, Luna proudly introduced her grandmother to Ms. Britt and her classmates. For the first time, Luna seemed to realize that she had stories others might be curious about and her stories would bring more questions—
it was easier to talk about things she knew.

Ms. Britt realized, too, that this quiet, hesitant child had a world she wanted to talk about if given the structure and permission to do so. Encouraging stories showed a side of Luna that had not been seen before. Because the stories helped her to learn more about her students, Ms. Britt made storytelling an integral part of her literacy curriculum.

Connecting Luna's Story to Resilience-Promoting Skills

Our students' identities are shaped both by their self-discovery and their experiences with the adults who care for them—parents, grandparents, aunts, uncles, teachers, and so on. As teachers, it's critical to remind ourselves that a child's identity begins with how her caregivers respond to her in every space of her life, including in our classrooms. When a child experiences warm, caring responses from her caregivers, she develops a positive emotional bond that promotes a positive sense of self. A child's identity is constantly being shaped as she interacts in the world, experiencing failures and successes.

Ms. Britt noticed that Luna was quiet and reserved and that Luna often sat alone and rarely engaged with others. As the only Spanish-speaking child in the classroom, Luna was aware and hesitant because she knew she was different from the other students and was not quite sure that her differences would be accepted. In fact, as children begin to understand themselves, they may become shy about asserting those parts of themselves they think others may perceive as different. But by asking Luna to share words in English and Spanish, Ms. Britt helped Luna to see that she could share her language and others would excitedly receive it (Espinoza & Ascenzi-Moreno, 2021). This affirmation allowed Luna to experience her classmates' curiosity about her as acceptance. When Ms. Britt saw Luna take the initial steps to share more about her *abuelita* and dog, she invited Luna to elaborate, and encouraged Luna to share the English meanings of the words *abuelita* and *dulce*. In this way, Ms. Britt helped Luna build self-confidence (emotional skill), and when she encouraged Luna to talk about herself using the language that is most familiar to her, she helped Luna to effectively communicate, another resilience-promoting skill. We saw how Luna, more at ease through this supported sharing, now willingly explored the map and looked at the photos her peers placed on the map. By the end of the day, when Luna's *abuelita* came to get her, she shared more stories about the people, places, and things that were most important to her. All of this was evidence of the beginning social skills that Luna was developing.

> *As teachers, it's critical to remind ourselves that a child's identity begins with how her caregivers respond to her in every space of her life, including in our classrooms.*

Tipping the Scale for Luna: Positive Self-Identity

The engagement that Ms. Britt provided offered Luna and her classmates an opportunity to share authentic stories about who they are and what matters to them. For Luna, this was the mirror that offered her a reflection of herself. This activity capitalized on the people, places, and things that Luna holds dear. As a result, she engaged in the activity and others learned some aspects of her identity that she hadn't revealed before. For them, this became a window that allowed them to see her. Rudine Sims Bishop (1990) reminds us that children need to see themselves reflected in the curriculum we use to teach them. Sims Bishop also reminds us that books are socializers and give subtle messages about what is truly valued in society. Storytelling, as woven into the map activity in Luna's class, also served as a sliding glass door—a portal to understanding that can be entered and exited as students learn more about each other and their worlds. To affirm Luna's language use continually in the classroom, Ms. Britt can read aloud texts that include more Spanish language, such as *ABeCedarios: Mexican Folk Art ABCs in English and Spanish* by Cynthia Weill, *Arroz con leche: Popular Songs and Rhymes from Latin America* by Lulu Delacre, and *¡Vámonos! Let's Go!* by René Colato Laínez.

Ms. Britt will use a combination of powerful texts and teaching strategies to affirm the lives of her students and their literacy development (Muhammad, 2023). Through her actions, she is tipping the scale by helping Luna share personal stories about herself and her family. She is gently giving Luna the capacity to bring voice to who she is, to her self-identity, and in this way, giving Luna a skill that shifts her fulcrum. Ms. Britt also supports Luna through this activity by minimizing any social comparisons that can cause Luna to feel inferior to others in her class. Having a positive self-identity will give Luna more confidence to handle new challenges. As Luna develops a stronger self-identity, what are some of the impacts on her social and academic life that Ms. Britt can look for and support? Luna may be willing to work harder to accomplish new goals and persevere even when she is not successful on the first, second, or third attempt. Through her hard work and determination, Luna may gain fortitude and start to see failures as learning opportunities, each key features of a stronger self-identity. Ms. Britt can cheer on Luna and her classmates as they learn that they can get back up and try again and again.

When the Scale Tips in the Negative Direction

A substantial body of research suggests that a low sense of self affects students' motivation and is a barrier to their learning (Green et al., 2006). When a child has a low sense of self, he or she may exhibit self-defeating behaviors such as avoidance, giving up easily, or being overly compliant. The child may find it hard to stand up for him- or herself, may be more vulnerable to teasing and bullying, and may have difficulties making and keeping friends. The child may feel anxious, depressed, frustrated, or sad. He or she may not be motivated to try new and challenging things for fear that the task at hand may be too difficult or because of self-imposed limitations. The child may constantly compare him- or herself to others and may even put him- or herself down when failing.

When students do not have affirming experiences in school, nor with enabling text, it can cause them tremendous distress that gets built into children's school personas—essentially limiting their ability to express themselves authentically—and may prevent them from becoming a seen and valued part of a classroom or school community. Alfred Tatum defines enabling texts as "text that moves beyond a sole cognitive focus—such as skill and strategy development—to include an academic, cultural, emotional, and social focus that moves students closer to examining issues they find relevant to their lives" (Tatum, 2009). In other words, Tatum suggests that children need exposure to texts that have real meaning for them, texts that pay attention to their multiple identities.

A substantial body of research suggests that a low sense of self affects students' motivation and is a barrier to their learning.

Bearing in mind all that is at stake for all students each day at school, we invite you to take proactive steps to help them build a strong sense of self and help them tip their resilience scales toward positive outcomes.

Identity Development Begins With a Child's Family

One of the most important things families can do is offer children positive affirmations of who they are and who they are becoming. Families can support children through this discovery and identity development process by offering guidance and giving them the freedom to learn on their own. As children age, they learn to understand the social meanings that are attached to an identity. When a child has a positive individual and group identity, he or she usually experiences a sense of belonging. When the child has a negative individual or group identity, the opposite is true. Families can serve as a buffer from the world and as a reflective mirror for a child to know who he or she truly is.

Positive Self-Identities in Our Literacy Classrooms and Beyond

The students we teach are complex, unique individuals. As a resilience-informed teacher, you want to help your students cultivate healthy self-identities and understand and know their true selves, and you want to do so without dehumanizing or devaluing others who may be different from who they are. These supports help students develop positive self-identity:

- Engaging in open conversations about a variety of topics and issues (with peers and in class discussions)

- Understanding they are valued by peers and caring adults who display a genuine concern for them. (In school, this includes everyone from school safety officers to classroom teachers!)

- Experiencing supportive relationships with both adults and peers

- Seeing that others with similar identities are valued and appreciated

- Having access to diverse classroom texts that do not limit students to one cultural story

Literature can serve as the windows, mirrors, and sliding glass doors (Bishop, 1990) that help children paint positive images of themselves and invite them into the worlds of others. Children benefit from seeing a wide range of people with different lived experiences through high-quality literature that is well-written and well-illustrated and captures the diverse and vibrant world we live in. The books that follow are a sampling of literature we find to be supportive of children's identity development.

Grades K–2

I Need a Hug / Necesito un abrazo **by Aaron Blabey** This bilingual tale from Aaron Blabey follows an adorable little porcupine looking for a hug. When his animal friends decline because of his prickly spikes, he becomes discouraged. That is, until he meets a slithering snake who has also been rejected by the animals and would absolutely love a hug! Porcupine and Snake show readers the importance of learning to accept who we are and the things that make us unique.

Me, Frida, and the Secret of the Peacock Ring **by Angela Cervantes** A celebration of culture and family ties, Angela Cervantes's novel would be a wonderful primary read-aloud. The story follows Paloma Marquez, a young girl traveling to Mexico City to connect with the birthplace of her deceased father. When Paloma meets two mysterious siblings who seek her help in finding a precious ring that belonged to beloved Mexican artist Frida Kahlo, she learns more about her Mexican heritage—and herself—than she ever anticipated.

You Are Enough: A Book About Inclusion **by Margaret O'Hair and Sofia Sanchez** This empowering picture book from author-illustrator team Margaret O'Hair and Sofia Cardoso is inspired by the real-life story of Sofia Sanchez—a young actress and model with Down syndrome. Through words of encouragement and a series of illustrations depicting children of different backgrounds, Sofia's message rings through—we can learn how special our identifies truly are if we only find the confidence to be "perfectly ourselves."

Grades 3–5

***Barakah Beats* by Maleeha Siddiqui** Nimra Sharif is faced with drastic changes and challenges as she transitions from her Islamic school to a public middle school. When her best friend begins distancing herself, visibly uncomfortable with Nimra's *hijab* and cultural practices, Nimra finds acceptance from an unlikely source—the popular 8th grade boy band, Bakarah Beats. As she navigates this new friendship, Nimra deals with the conflict between her passion for the band and her religion. Debut-author Maleeha Siddiqui's book highlights the importance of advocating for what you believe in and the joys of embracing your truest self.

***I Color Myself Different* by Colin Kaepernick** This ode to the beauty and importance of Black and Brown children is based on a defining moment in Colin Kaepernick's life: a school assignment to draw a portrait of his family. Colin colors himself with a brown crayon, which sets him apart from his family members and prompts endless inquiries from his classmates. Remembering the wisdom his mother shared about how special our differences are, he teaches the class a powerful lesson about embracing your identity and loving yourself.

***The Many Colors of Harpreet Singh* by Supriya Kelkar** Supriya Kelkar and Alea Marley's colorful story follows Harpreet Singh, a young boy with a passion for picking just the right color *patka*, or turban, to match his mood. When his family relocates to a snowy city across the country, he finds it increasingly difficult to express himself in a new environment. He tries to rely on his white turban with the hope of blending in, but a newfound friendship and the quick arrival of spring helps Harpreet embrace who he is and reminds readers about the true beauty of being seen.

Summary of Key Points

- Identity development is a lifelong journey that begins with a child's awareness that he or she is a separate, unique individual with physical, social, emotional, and cognitive needs and wants.

- A child constantly receives messages from those in his or her environment that impacts that development.

- When a child has a positive sense of self, he or she tends to meet challenges and adversities with a strong sense of agency—and also knows how to ask others for help when needed.

As resilience-informed educators, we play an important role in our students' lives. We can support a healthy sense of identity through our curriculum and the resources we use to teach and engage them.

In the pages that follow are some classroom-tested ways that resilience-informed teachers can use their literacy curriculum to cultivate a child's sense of self. You'll see that the four skills groups we discussed in Chapter 1—emotional skills, social skills, communication skills, and executive function skills—are woven throughout the routines and activities.

ROUTINES AND ACTIVITIES TO FORM POSITIVE SELF-IDENTITIES

	Routines and Activities	Social Skill	Emotional Skill	Communication Skill	Executive Function Skill	Page Number
ROUTINES	One-of-a-Kind Greetings	●	●	●		71
	Intergenerational Storytelling Projects		●	●		71
	Classroom Library Audit	●			●	71
ACTIVITIES	Identity Web: Who Am I?	●	●	●	●	72
	Pieces of a Puzzle	●	●	●		74
	Dear Selfie Journal				●	76
	Letter to My Future Self		●		●	78

☐ **One-of-a-Kind Greetings**

Let each student decide on a unique way to greet you at the door each morning or when the class gathers on the rug. Invite students to say "good morning" the way their families say it, make a special gesture of welcome, or come up with a new way to say or show, "I'm here."

☐ **Intergenerational Storytelling Projects**

Families and communities have a long legacy and rich history of stories that can be passed on from one generation to the next. The stories can relate shared cultural legacies, values, lessons about the ways we treat one another, humorous reminders and guiding principles, and historical roots. Have students interact with older members of their families and community and ask to hear their stories. Encourage families to capture intergenerational stories in written, audio, and visual forms, so they can be stored for repeated listening and for future generations. (Be mindful that family composition comes in a variety of formats, and that when defining families, you will want children to understand that families are the biological and nonbiological caring individuals with whom children identify.)

☐ **Classroom Library Audit**

Your classroom collection can support students' identity formation when your students have access to books that serve as mirrors, reflecting their own lives and languages, as well as to books that serve as windows and sliding glass doors, expanding their knowledge about the identities of others. Start reviewing the books on your shelves (students can be invited to review them, too!). Note the characters and situations in the books. Will students find any books featuring characters with lives and families like theirs? What cultures are represented across your collection? To enrich your collection, work with a librarian to look for age-appropriate literature from diverse cultures and books representing linguistic differences (collections such as Rising Voices and Our Voices from Scholastic can provide a range of own-voices authors and illustrators telling stories about their own cultures). (Adapted from *Revolutionary Love*, Wynter-Hoyte et al., 2022.)

Identity Web: Who Am I?

A great way to get to know your students at the start of the year, Identity Webs help students articulate the factors that shape who they are—from favorite foods and hobbies to home languages. This activity can help children build confidence as they share what matters most to them. At the same time, sharing can spark curiosity and build empathy, creating the potential for stronger bonds among classmates and breaking down stereotypes.

FORMAT: Small or whole group

1. **Model creating an Identity Web with a center circle and four to six radiating circles.** Start with your picture or name in the center circle and write or draw your interests and experiences in the radiating circles. As you go, think aloud to show how you select your interests, characteristics, hobbies, and so on.

2. **Invite students to create a web of their own.** Circulate and confer with students, offering guidance as needed.

3. **Ask students to share their completed webs with the group or class.** Encourage active listening and celebrate how students learned important new things about one another.

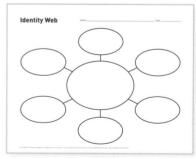

Go to scholastic.com/resilience-resources for an Identity Web template.

Adding words and illustrations to an Identity Web tells a personal story.

TIPS

FOR GRADES K–2: Consider the experiences and things that kids this age love (e.g., their favorite food, color, things they like to do, and people or animals they love). You might think aloud as you fill in your selections, "Mangoes are my favorite fruit. I'm going to draw a picture of a mango in one of my circles. The kinds of foods I love tell you something about me."

FOR GRADES 3–5: As you model and prompt, encourage students to think beyond favorite things to important cultural aspects of their lives (e.g., things they like to do with their families, places they like to visit, cultural groups they belong to, or languages they speak). You might think aloud, "I'm going to write 'taking hikes' in this circle. Being outdoors and hiking is important to me. I think of myself as a hiker. It's part of who I am," or, "In this circle, I'll write that I'm bilingual. I speak English and Spanish."

Pieces of a Puzzle

If we consider the numerous aspects that make up our "whole" personalities, we may notice that these aspects resemble individual puzzle pieces. However, creating a sturdy puzzle with pieces that fit together can be challenging and children may need help drawing, cutting, and piecing back together the pieces to make the whole. This activity is a great way to help students identify the interests, familial, or cultural factors that contribute to creating an identity that is "whole" and unique to an individual. By "puzzling out" the identity of a famous person first and then curating their own personal puzzle pieces, students can understand how complex identities are—as well as build empathy and a deeper appreciation for the unique identities of those around them.

FORMAT: Small group or individual

1. **Partner with your school or local librarian to gather and book-talk biographies of people from many cultures and career paths that students will be able to read.**

2. **Group students and invite each group to select a contemporary or historical figure they've read about who interests them.** Have them draw or download, resize, and print a letter-sized image of the figure.

3. **Have them consider four to six aspects of this person's identity for creating their puzzle.** Lists of character traits (curious, brave, justice-oriented) can be a good reference. Older students may want to focus on four to six aspects of the person's life experience that influenced them, such as family, friends, interests and hobbies, culture, religion, and opportunities.

4. **To make the puzzle, have students cut up the picture into four to six pieces.** On the back of each piece, have students write about (or draw a picture describing) one aspect of the person's identity.

5. **Invite students to repeat the exercise individually, using themselves as the subject.** Ask them to write or draw aspects of their own identities on the back of the puzzle pieces. Encourage students to think of parallels between the types

of traits they wrote about (or drew) of the historical figure and themselves.

6. Puzzles can be stored in resealable plastic bags and circulated to families so meaningful discussions about all the figures the class has studied can be shared at home, too.

TIPS

FOR GRADES K–2: You may find it helpful to guide a younger group with questions throughout the activity that can clarify what they are meant to write on their puzzle pieces. It may be easier for them at this age to conceptualize their identity if they are prompted to list the things they (or the person they're learning about) love, which can range from favorite foods, favorite media, or colors they love to an animal or person that is important to them.

FOR GRADES 3–5: At this age, students will be able to identify more complex aspects of identity, like cultural backgrounds, languages spoken, hobbies, etc. Encourage students to consider what makes them unique in their day-to-day lives, and why they have chosen to write down each aspect. When sharing with one another, invite students to remark on what they found interesting or something they have in common with another classmate's puzzle piece.

Dear Selfie Journal

Journaling can be a great way for students to organize their thoughts and reflect on their past, current, and future selves. By assigning journaling topics like those shared below, you will help students think about the private and public parts of self that everyone experiences. By writing about themselves and sharing their thinking and writing with others, students build self-awareness and confidence and put their communication skills into practice.

FORMAT: Whole class, small group, and individual

Discuss with students the different ways we can think about our identities. Let them know that we can focus our thoughts by categorizing them. Introduce some identity-focused categories such as those listed below and share example questions.

How I See Myself

- What three words would you use to describe yourself and why?
- What makes you unique?
- What do you love about yourself?
- What do you most want someone to know about you?

How Others See Me

- What three words might people use to describe you?
- What are some of the nice things people have said about you?

Things About Me Others Can't See

- What is something that people would be surprised to learn about you?
- What is something no one knows about you?

Where I Belong

- Describe your community. Who lives there? What are some of your favorite parts of your community?

1. **Before students write in their Dear Selfie Journals, have them ask each other some questions that fall under the different categories.** You may have them do this as a turn-and-talk, in small groups, or taking turns as a whole class. Guide students to notice the types of things they learn about each other depending upon the type of questions they ask—what is revealed, their private selves or their public selves? Do these overlap?

2. **Provide students with journals (or have students create their own with recycled paper) to serve as their "Dear Selfie Journal" for the marking period or school year.** You may invite them to decorate it in a way that represents their personalities.

3. **Dedicate consistent time each week for journal entries.** Encourage students to use the guiding questions you provided, but also allow them to veer off and write about what interests them.

4. **Give students the option to share parts of their journal entries with the classmate next to them.** Remember to explain that this step is optional and that it's completely okay if they don't feel comfortable sharing their writing.

5. **Carve out time to read journal entries on a regular basis, making sure students are comfortable with you reading their writing.** This is a great way to learn more about your students and how to best support them.

TIPS

FOR GRADES K–2: You can adapt the topics above to fit a younger group of students. It may be helpful to begin with journal prompts that ask them to describe their favorites or current hobbies/interests.

FOR GRADES 3–5: You can adapt the topics above to fit an older group of students, if needed.

Letter to My Future Self

Writing a letter to their future selves is a great way for students to reflect on what they love about themselves now and to think about the characteristics or skills they want to acquire or develop. Students' acknowledgment of their current strengths serves as the scaffolding for setting future goals and aspirations.

FORMAT: Individual

1. Announce to the class that you have secured a time capsule (a large envelope or shoe box) and that there's space for each student to add a letter to their future selves to be read at a certain date (end of the school year tends to work well).

2. **Using a 3-2-1 Organizer, invite students to list three things they admire about themselves or feel grateful for being able to do, two things in the world that bring them joy, and one thing they would like to improve or learn how to do by the time they open their letters.** You may want to have students share their ideas with partners to help them describe their ideas in more detail before they write.

Go to scholastic.com/resilience-resources for a 3-2-1 Organizer template.

Name _____ Date _____

321 Organizer

3 3 things I admire about myself

1. _____
_____
2. _____
_____
3. _____
_____

2 2 things that bring me joy

1. _____
_____
2. _____
_____

1 1 thing I'd like to improve or learn how to do

_____
_____

3. **Have students use the ideas they've generated to compose a letter addressed to their future selves.** This is a good opportunity to model an informal letter structure. To engage them in writing to their audience, ask them to imagine their future selves reading the letter—how they look and where they are reading it.

4. **Gather the letters in the time capsule and store or lock the box in a special cabinet or drawer until it's time to open it.** Mark the date on your class calendar and plan a letter-opening event where students may read their letters and write a reflection about their evolving traits, joys, and goals.

TIPS

FOR GRADES K–2: If students need a lot of assistance with letter writing, consider either co-creating a letter template with students, leaving spaces for them to fill in their ideas in their own letters, or making the 3-2-1 Organizer the page students send to their future selves.

FOR GRADES 3–5: This letter activity can be made digital for older students with more technology experience on websites like FutureMe.org, where students can write a letter to their future selves and receive it by email on the date they choose.

CHAPTER 4

SUPPORTING CURIOSITY AND MOTIVATION

"The important thing is not to stop questioning. Curiosity has its own reason for existing."

—Albert Einstein

W hat is the most intriguing question you have ever been asked? What is the one question you have yet to find an answer to that would satisfy a curiosity? When was the last time you felt curious about something? What motivates you to learn more? When you were a child, how did your teachers and family members respond when you asked questions? How do you respond when your students ask you questions? What questions are on your mind at this moment?

You may be wondering, why all the questions? Questions are important. They are evidence of a curious mind. Curiosity motivates us to explore, discover, figure things out, and find answers. Our curiosity leads to learning. Just like us, our students are also curious; they ask lots of questions. You've probably fielded questions of all types from students, including questions that stem from children's need to:

- acquire information about nature and the way things work, such as "Why did that lizard change colors?" and "How many stars are in the universe?"

- discuss spiritual questions and what it means to be human, such as "Where do people go when they die?" and "Why can't I fly like a bird?"

- be reassured about their safety and well-being, such as "What can we do to help our planet?" and "Who can I talk to if I have a problem?"

Some of their questions are easy to answer, some are more difficult, and for some, no answer is ever sufficient. Some of the questions stem from children's natural curiosity and their desire for information. Others stem from their fears and worries. When we listen and intentionally respond, we can promote a learning mindset in our students. By doing so, we support them as curious meaning-makers who comprehend that there are always different ways of seeing and understanding people, events, and generally the world around us. Cultivating a curious mindset is also an important resilience-promoting skill. When we can pause, look around, reflect, and ask questions such as, "How could she do this to me?"; "Why did he say that?"; "Why did that just happen?"; "What am I missing that would help me understand this person better?"; and so forth, we are using a curiosity mindset to help us navigate often challenging, even stressful circumstances. Cultivating that mindset in our students so that they more naturally use this skill in their day-to-day lives gives them an important tool for making sense of events, behaviors, and circumstances that may initially seem overwhelming.

What Does It Mean to Be Curious?

Markey and Loewenstein (2014) define curiosity as the desire for knowledge. It is the gap between what we know and what we desire to know, and the motivation to fill this gap. Research confirms that curiosity leads to higher academic outcomes. For example, in a recent study, Shah et al. (2018) found a connection between greater curiosity and higher levels of reading and math in kindergarten children. Others have found a link between curiosity and higher academic performance on standardized tests (Wavo, 2004), and that curiosity enhances one's ability to learn and retain new information (Kang, et al., 2009; Gruber, et al., 2014). When children are curious about a topic, they are more likely to remember the information they learn about the topic. Research shows that seeking knowledge to satisfy our curiosity activates the reward center of our brains (Kang et al., 2009). There is an emotional response. When we satisfy our curiosity, it feels really good. Imagine the immense joy that children feel when they figure out the answer to an issue they have been grappling with the last few days and the joy that spills forth when they laugh and say, "Now I see!"

When children are curious about a topic, they are more likely to remember the information they learn about the topic. Research shows that seeking knowledge to satisfy our curiosity activates the reward center of our brains.

Curiosity and Our Social Worlds

People who are curious often benefit from social encounters—or, at least, curious people fare better socially. Recent studies suggest that curious people are viewed in social situations as more interesting and engaging, better able to connect with strangers, and less aggressive (Kashdan et al., 2013; Kashdan & Steger, 2007). Curious people interact better with others in social situations and are less defensive when responding to existential threats (Kashdan et al., 2011; Kashdan & Roberts, 2004).

Studies also show that mindful and curious people are more receptive to information that may challenge the personal beliefs and cultural values they hold. In a study conducted in Japan, researchers found that participants who were more curious were less affected by social rejection, experienced more satisfaction in life, and were less depressed than those who were less curious (Kawamoto et al., 2017). People who are curious are also better able to think flexibly. We will explore the concept of flexible thinking more in depth in Chapter 5.

Shifting the Fulcrum Through Curiosity and Motivation

Curiosity and motivation go hand in hand. Individuals who are curious are usually highly motivated to learn and vice versa. Those who are highly motivated are often curious. Motivation is powered by our desires and ambitions, but mostly by our curiosities. When a child is curious, he or she has an intense motivation to "engage in persistent information-seeking behavior" (Shin & Kim, 2019). When children are fascinated by a topic, they will devour everything they can about that topic. Children who are fascinated with astronomy may read everything on the topic they can get their hands on, watch any number of space-related videos, and save up to buy themselves a telescope to explore the night sky. Motivation is the driving force that pushes children to take action to accomplish something that is important to them. Motivation is powered by their desires and ambition but most importantly, by curiosity. When we encourage our students to be curious and to follow their interests, we are supportive of the positive shifts they can make in life.

As a demonstration of this, we will share the story of Mrs. Ellen Lopez, a teacher who got her students motivated to explore their curiosity by thinking about the people who once lived on the land where they now play.

BUILDING CHILDREN'S CURIOSITY:
Mrs. Lopez's Story

Mrs. Lopez, a third-grade teacher in Arizona, had recently noticed a challenge among her students. She was having difficulty getting them to talk in class and was trying to think of ways to help build their communication and storytelling skills. She was looking for something outside her regular curriculum to spark their curiosity and get them motivated. As she was trying to think of an original approach, she heard about a project organized by a documentary photographer named Stephen Alvarez, who was working on something called the Mural of America project that explored different North American cultural landmarks that illuminate the complex artistic mysteries of the past. Stephen was photographing cave drawings made thousands of years ago by indigenous people living across America. One of those sites was in the same community where Mrs. Lopez was teaching now. Mrs. Lopez was suddenly struck with inspiration. Why not spark her students' interest in stories by teaching them about an ancient form of storytelling: cave painting? She reached out to Stephen and together they developed a curriculum to teach third graders about the indigenous communities who lived on the land where her students now played.

How could they get the third graders excited to learn about those who lived on their land thousands of years earlier and to make connections between the lives of these people and their own? Mrs. Lopez came up with an idea to introduce her students to ancient history by immersing them in a project that would engage their imagination and connect them to the past. She decided to have her students reenact the ancient art of cave painting. But first, she piqued their curiosity with a short online film presentation about the cave drawings Stephen had recorded with his camera by crawling through narrow spaces deep in the ground. Mrs. Lopez then asked her students to crawl under their desks on their backs. She had taped white paper to the underside of each desk and put a few crayons under the desks.

Continued from previous page

She closed the blinds and turned the lights off in the classroom. Each student had a tiny flashlight with just a glimmer of light. She asked them to draw something they would like future students to know was important to them.

The exercise was a success. Her students were able to talk about the stories they'd drawn in their own "caves" about their own lives. Excited by their own stories, they wondered about the stories that were illustrated in ancient times. They were filled with questions about what these ancient people had drawn, who they were, and how they had lived. The project ignited her students' curiosity as they learned about the past and worked on stories of their own for future generations.

Connecting Mrs. Lopez's Story to Resilience-Promoting Skills

By asking her students to place themselves in ancient times by making their own "cave drawings," Mrs. Lopez ignited her students' curiosity. Now, history was something they could understand. It wasn't just an old story about people long ago, which didn't always interest her third graders. Instead, she was able to demonstrate to her students how the ancient people who drew on cave walls were much like themselves. And that all people had stories to tell. The students were much more interested in learning about the indigenous cultures of these people who once inhabited the land the more they realized how alike they were. By making the lesson personal, Mrs. Lopez gave her students a reason to want to seek out more information. She brought storytelling to life. Now her students had loads of questions about the people who once lived on the land where they now lived, worked, and played.

Tipping the Scale for Mrs. Lopez's Students: Curiosity as a Motivator

When students are curious, they are motivated to take risks and try novel things. The classroom communities that we create either encourage or discourage our learners to be curious. We support our students' curiosity when we honor their questions, support their interests, provide time for them to construct their own knowledge, and teach them to question the answers given.

Honor Their Questions: Our questions push us to think deeply. Encouraging children to ask questions that require more than just a "yes" or "no" or simple sentence response and teaching them how to seek their own answers supports their curiosity. We can cultivate wonderment in our students when we honor their questions. When children ask questions and we respond thoughtfully to their inquiries, we affirm for our students that it is okay to want to learn more. It is also important that when we don't know the answer to a question, we model for them how to search for the answer.

Support Their Interests: Find out which topics excite your students and weave them into your lessons. Using students' interests to build curricula, when appropriate, supports their learning and engagement and cuts down on negative behaviors that often result from boredom and lack of stimulation.

Provide Time for Them to Construct Their Own Knowledge: When children are actively engaged and invested in what they are being taught, they tend to learn more. We are supportive of them when we infuse our classroom community with novelties and our curriculum with engaging materials for our students to experience and investigate as they construct their own knowledge. We also support them when we praise and encourage them for figuring things out on their own.

Teach Them to Question the Answers: Teach your students that they do not always need to accept an answer at face value. It's important for them to know how an answer was reached and if there are alternative answers that are just as viable. This will require them to investigate the answers they have been given.

When the Scale Tips in the Negative Direction

Most children live with a sense of wonderment; they are curious. That is, until we teach them not to be. We dissuade our students' curiosity when we discourage them from asking too many questions, create classroom communities that rely heavily on teacher-directed learning and predetermined learning outcomes, and when time for student exploration is limited.

Discouraging Their Questions: When we do not respond or when we respond in a manner that signals to children that their questions are not important, we inadvertently teach them to ask fewer and fewer questions and to be less and less inquisitive about the world around them. Additionally, when we don't address questions that reflect students' deep concerns and fears, those worries may show up as anxiety and detract from their ability to learn.

Teacher-directed Learning and Predetermined Learning Outcomes: In classroom communities that are heavily teacher-directed or learning happens through a "sit and get" format, children are less inquisitive and less likely to explore a range of topics that may be of interest to them. Our curriculum should be student-centered so that our learners are fully engaged in learning what is being taught.

Limited Time for Exploration: Children learn through play and active participation. We also dissuade our students' curiosity when we do not allow them time to explore topics of interest. We offer several strategies at the end of this chapter that can be used to promote active learning.

Families Supporting a Child's Curiosity at Home

Supportive caregivers can encourage a child's innate curiosity. They can reinforce curiosity when they see it in action. When a child asks, "why, how, or what if," a caregiver can acknowledge the child's questions and encourage the child to investigate and explore those questions in depth through play. When children play, they can be encouraged to explore new things. It is important for families to admit when they don't know something, wonder out loud, and model curious thinking

for children to emulate. This helps children understand that learning is a never-ending process. Creating situations or asking questions to guide a child to use his or her executive functioning skills is also helpful. Providing novelty experiences for children may also motivate them to be curious. For instance, if a child loves the beach, a trip to the shore or an aquarium may offer a novel experience to explore ocean life that he or she may be unfamiliar with.

Curiosity and Motivation in Our Literacy Classrooms and Beyond

Instilling in every student the desire to learn is what every teacher hopes to accomplish. Curiosity-driven learning and intrinsic motivation are fundamental components of efficient education (Freeman et al., 2014; Ryan & Deci, 2000).

Curiosity-driven learning and intrinsic motivation are fundamental components of efficient education.

Instilling in every student the desire to learn is what every teacher hopes to accomplish. When intrinsic motivation and curiosity are missing, engagement falters. Researchers have found that when teachers arouse students' curiosity about something they're naturally motivated to learn, students are better prepared to learn things that they would normally consider boring or difficult. When Mrs. Lopez worked with the photographer to engage her students in creative ways, she motivated their curiosity and soon discovered that students had endless questions. They were intrinsically motivated to learn more about the indigenous people who lived in their community so long ago, and it excited them to think about how their own lives might be seen by people far in the future.

We can arouse our students' motivation by stocking our libraries with books that match the topic interests and genres they currently enjoy, as well as with robust book sets on topics you'll study as a class. Below we offer books about curiosity and classroom-tested activities to help you pique your students' curious minds.

Grades K–2

Ada Twist, Scientist by Andrea Beaty The ever-
inquisitive young Ada is always in pursuit of answers.
On the hunt to find the source of a stinky smell, Ada
inadvertently creates chaos and tries her parents'
patience along the way. But that doesn't stop her
from following her passion and eventually winning
over her parents. Told in rhyme, the story of Ada
illustrates the rewards of following one's curiosity.

Everywhere, Wonder by Matthew Swanson
Through a young narrator with a talent for finding
beauty in the simplest of moments, author Matthew Swanson
and illustrator Robbi Behr unveil the endless wonders
hidden in the corners of our world. Whether it's uncovering
the bustling life lurking under the freezing waters of Alaska
or investigating the origins of a single noodle in a bowl of
soup, readers are invited to notice and stay curious about the
wonders that surround them.

The Girl With Big, Big Questions by Britney Winn Lee
In their story about an inquisitive young girl, author
Britney Winn Lee and illustrator Jacob Souva encourage
children to celebrate their curious minds. On her quest
to uncover answers to questions like, "Why can't people
live on the moon?" or "Why does bedtime exist?" the
young girl soon becomes discouraged when people
grow tired of her persistent questions. However, her
genius idea to find a home for a fallen bird's nest
teaches those around her that the gift of curiosity is
exactly what helps us grow.

Grades 3–5

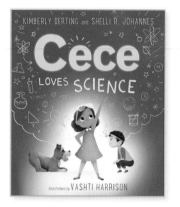

Cece Loves Science *by Kimberly Derting and Shelli R. Johannes*
Everyone knows Cece loves to ask questions, especially her teacher who thinks becoming a scientist will be the perfect career for her. When Cece and her best friend are assigned a science project, they conduct experiments to determine if Cece's dog, Einstein, will eat vegetables. This picture book from Kimberly Derting and Shelli R. Johannes, illustrated by Vashti Harrison, celebrates girls in STEM and teaches readers that even though science can feel like an endless series of questions, having the motivation to find answers leads to exciting results!

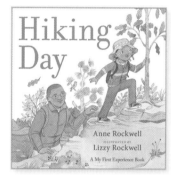

Hiking Day *by Anne Rockwell* During an autumn hike on Hickory Hill with her parents, a young girl is mesmerized by the picture-perfect landscape. Equipped with her trusty floppy hat and sturdy sneakers, the young girl pays close attention to the crunching leaves, towering trees, and even meets new animal friends along the way to the summit. Author-illustrator team Anne and Lizzy Rockwell bring to life a story about the joys of being curious about the world and its simple pleasures.

Just Ask! Be Different, Be Brave, Be You *by Sonia Sotomayor* Inspired by her diabetes diagnosis at seven years old, Supreme Court Justice Sonia Sotomayor's picture book celebrates children's curiosity and encourages them to "just ask" about the things they may not understand. Rafael López's illustrations introduce readers to several children—one who needs an inhaler, one with ADHD, and another who needs to take insulin to keep herself healthy. By learning about their lives, readers are reminded that our differences are also precisely what make the world interesting.

Summary of Key Points

- Humans have a natural capacity for curiosity that emerges in childhood; by encouraging students to ask questions and seek solutions to daily challenges, we increase their capacity to draw on their questioning and problem-solving skills in the face of adversity.

- Our curiosity motivates us to actively learn new and challenging things.

- Our curiosity is piqued by our passions.

- When we are curious about something, we are more likely to become intensely focused on learning, especially when it is something that is meaningful to our lives.

- A resilience-informed teacher knows that when students are motivated, curious, passionate about what they are learning, and have opportunities to collaborate and learn with and from each other, curiosity increases.

- A resilience-informed teacher, prepares his or her students to ask questions that may lead them to more adaptive behaviors and solutions.

In the pages that follow, we provide classroom-tested routines and activities that resilience-informed teachers can use to help foster curiosity and motivation daily. The four skill groups are woven throughout the routines and activities.

ROUTINES AND ACTIVITIES TO BUILD CURIOSITY AND MOTIVATION

Routines and Activities		Social Skill	Emotional Skill	Communication Skill	Executive Function Skill	Page Number
ROUTINES	Model Curiosity	•	•	•	•	95
	Acknowledge and Reward Curiosity	•	•	•		95
	Reflect on Curiosity and Motivation	•	•	•	•	95
ACTIVITIES	Show and Tell With Quality Questions		•	•	•	96
	Curiosity Chronicles: Family Stories			•	•	98
	Booktalking Favorite Books			•	•	100
	Using QFT: Questions Formulation Technique	•		•	•	102

☐ **Model Curiosity**

Model your curiosity for your students. When you are intrigued by something, you can think aloud so that children understand your thought processes and the kinds of questions you ask.

☐ **Acknowledge and Reward Curiosity**

When you notice that a student's inquiries and investigations are leading to his or her learning, acknowledge it during that learning and not only when the student earns a desired grade or achieves the desired outcome. In this way, you are instilling in him or her that effort is just as important as the outcome.

☐ **Reflect on Curiosity and Motivation**

A curious mind reflects regularly, seeking improvement. Consider these questions to evaluate whether your classroom environment and instruction are encouraging active learning for students:

- Are children engaging cognitively, emotionally, and/or physically with what they're learning?
- Are there opportunities for student choice in the lesson or activity?
- What are moments when students can lead the learning?
- Is feedback timely and specific?
- What student responses indicate they are ready to learn more—or go in a different direction?

Show and Tell With Quality Questions

"Show and Tell" is not only reserved for early childhood spaces—older students can also benefit from sharing items that are special to them and represent their personality. Expand upon a typical show-and-tell experience by helping students engage each presenter with quality, open-ended questions about their artifact. In this way, students engage in active listening so they can build upon the information that's being shared.

Format: Whole group

1. **Ask students to bring in an item that is connected to a cultural or community group to which they belong—groups can include broad categories like ethnicity or nationality, or smaller communities, like being a member of a sports team or a club.**

2. **Have students sit in a circle and share their items one at a time.** You may choose to model the presentation by bringing in your own item and demonstrating what this activity will look like.

3. **Explain to students that they can learn more about the special items and why they're so important in their classmates' lives by asking open-ended questions.** You might provide some question stems for them, such as "Why did…"; "How did you know…"; and "What's the meaning behind…". Keep discussion focused on the connection between the student, the item, and the community it's linked to.

4. **Allow time for students to ask the presenter some open-ended questions about the artifact being shared.** Steer students away from yes or no questions. Remind them to listen carefully so that they may formulate a question that expands upon what they've heard. This is what active listening is all about.

5. **Discuss some of the surprising things that were learned when presenters answered classmates' inquires.** Help students to notice how thoughtful questions lead to interesting information.

TIPS

FOR GRADES K–2: It may be helpful to model a few standard open-ended questions students can ask each presenter, such as "Why did you choose this item?"; "How did you learn about it?"; and "What does this item mean to you?" These questions can help structure the presentation for younger students. Once they have the hang of it, encourage them to begin constructing open-ended questions of their own.

FOR GRADES 3–5: Reinforce the connection between questions and answers by having students write a reflection about one of the stories that emerged about their classmates' items, which might then be delivered to the presenter. Or, you may ask them to write a reflection on the item they shared, describing some things they may not have thought about until they were asked to elaborate.

Curiosity Chronicles: Family Stories

Collecting oral histories is a complex task that requires many skills to come into play. As students learn how to get older relatives to tell stories, they sharpen their communication and listening skills while building their understanding of storytelling. The interview format gives structure to expressing curiosity.

Format: Small or whole group

1. **To introduce the activity, explain that students will have the chance to interview a family member or close family friend about the history of their families.** You might suggest that students select an elder family member as their subject. Family-centered activities need to be approached with a delicate awareness that many different family circumstances exist—some students may have been adopted, some may be in foster care, and others may have a turbulent past. It's important to emphasize that every child has a rich story with support systems that makes them who they are. Encourage students to consider any important adult (including a school staff member) in their life as an interview subject.

2. **Help students work together to construct a list of interview questions that can be used to learn more about their families—these can include topics like cultural background, notable events and achievements, and personal anecdotes.** Talk to them about how the types of questions they ask will yield different kinds of responses. Encourage them to gather both factual details and personal opinions or feelings.

3. **Have students take the questions home with them and schedule the interview with their subject.** Be sure to remind them to take notes about what they learned and fill in answers to questions they drafted.

4. **When the interviews are complete, invite students to share their findings with the class.** Encourage active listening and ask students to provide comments on what they learned about the family member interviewed.

Starter Interview Questions

- What was a challenging moment for you when you were growing up? How did you handle it?
- Who did you look up to when you were my age and why?
- What was a proud moment for you in your life?
- What's a favorite memory you have of spending time with your family growing up?
- How did you choose my name?

TIPS

FOR GRADES K–2: It may be helpful to model a mock interview for younger students so they can have a point of reference. Be sure to practice in class ahead of the assignment due date and invite students to interview each other as "test subjects." You may choose to ask the adults in their lives to help conduct the interview and assist them in jotting down answers.

FOR GRADES 3–5: Rather than write responses to the interview questions, students can use multimedia (video or audio recording) to conduct the interview. Have them share the recordings with the class and invite students to share what they found interesting.

Booktalking Favorite Books

Oftentimes when we finish a good book, the first thing we want to do is tell our friends about it so they can enjoy it, too. As students take turns presenting their book recommendations, they learn to communicate effectively and engage in active listening. They also discover the excitement of an entire class brimming with enthusiasm for books, and they learn that they can inspire others with their authentic feelings.

Format: Small or whole group

1. **Have students select a favorite book—this may be a book they're reading independently, from a read-aloud in class, or other shared reading.**

2. **Ask them to create a list of what they like about the book.** The list could be related to themes, fascinating facts, memories they associate with the book, or personality traits in a character they relate to.

3. **On a separate day, invite students to present their favorite book and share their list of reasons for choosing the book as their favorite.** Encourage presenters to get their classmates interested in reading the book themselves. During the presentations, have students keep track of books that sound interesting to them. These short booktalks can be done over

Booktalk Tips

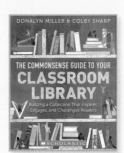

- Jot down a few key points on a sticky note to help you remember what you want to say.
- Share what you enjoyed about the book.
- Keep talks short and lively. Think of a booktalk as a commercial for the book.
- Visit Colby Sharp's YouTube channel to watch his recent booktalks as a model.

(Courtesy of Donalyn Miller and Colby Sharp, authors of *The Commonsense Guide to Your Classroom Library*)

time as students finish books, so booktalking becomes a frequent part of your reading routine.

4. **Create a class chart that lists the favorite book each student presented followed by some key reasons the book was chosen.** Students can refer to the chart the next time they're looking for a book to read. If they enjoyed the book as well, they can add their name to the class chart.

5. **Encourage students to continue to offer their classmates book recommendations they think they would like.** Have them add the title to the class chart and/or to their personal lists.

TIPS

FOR GRADES K–2: You might scaffold the booktalk as a question-and-answer format at first. It may be helpful to provide open-ended questions for each presenter to guide them toward identifying themes, fascinating facts, associated memories, or character traits. Follow up with students to encourage them to use their to-read list when selecting books.

FOR GRADES 3–5: You can extend the activity by asking older children to form book clubs based on similar interests. Book club members select a book to read and then meet to discuss it according to a schedule (e.g., twice a week, after having read to a stopping point determined by the group for each meeting). Have book club members keep track of the questions and ideas that came up. Check in with groups to find out how their conversations are both answering questions and raising new ones. This is a great opportunity to remind them that discussions with other readers about the same text often lead us to new questions and ways of seeing ideas and situations.

Using QFT: Questions Formulation Technique

When we teach students how to question, we empower them to become active learners. This simplified version of the Questions Formulation Technique puts decision-making skills into practice while also building self-awareness and confidence by letting students know that their interests matter.

Format: Small group or whole class

1. **Show students the cover of a picture book they have not read and have them ask as many questions as they can think of that the cover inspires.**

2. **Do not stop to judge, discuss, edit, or answer any of the questions.** If you're working with a small group or whole class, have students write down their own questions. Make sure students understand that they should write everything as it comes to mind without change. The idea is to brainstorm freely.

Example chart
from a K–2 class

> **Our Questions**
>
> ★ Who is Hermit Crab?
>   Where does Hermit Crab live?
> ★ Why does Hermit Crab need a house?
>   Where will the house be?
>   Does Hermit Crab have a family?
>   Does Hermit Crab have friends?
> ★ What happens to Hermit Crab?

3. Once they've recorded all their questions, have students choose three questions from their list that they are most curious to think about.

4. Then share the book as a read-aloud or have students read it independently.

5. After the read-aloud, ask students to reflect on whether their questions were answered by reading the book. Ask if there are any other ways they could find answers to their questions. This activity helps students gain practice and improve their ability to formulate meaningful questions that will guide their learning.

TIPS

FOR GRADES K–2: With younger students, you might teach this as a whole-class activity. You may go around the room and have each student contribute a question, which you can record on chart paper. At the end of the read-aloud, revisit the chart and discuss how each student's question made it interesting to read to find out.

FOR GRADES 3–5: Before students select their top questions, have them mark their questions as open-ended or closed, with a "c" or "o." Discuss the difference between the two types of questions and the purposes of each. Have students choose two closed questions and two open-ended questions. After the read-aloud, discuss the different things they learned from the two types of questions. Make sure students understand that one is not better than the other—both types of questions are valuable and useful.

CHAPTER 5

ENGAGING FLEXIBLE THINKING

"Give up the thought that you have control. You don't. The best you can do is adapt, anticipate, be flexible, sense the environment, and respond."

—Frances Arnold

I f you are like us, at some point in your career, you have worked with a colleague or two who have made the following statements or behaved in the following manner. Do any of these words and actions sound familiar?

What they might say:

- I don't want to do it that way.

- I already tried that.

- Why can't we just do it my way and be done with it?

- Why do things have to change? I hate change.

What they might do:

- have trouble maintaining emotional balance when there are last-minute changes

- express frustration any time they have to adjust and adapt

- see things only from their own perspective

In contrast, you've likely also worked with at least a few colleagues who have approached similar challenges quite differently.

What they might say:

- Let's try to do it that way, but if that doesn't work, we can try something else.

- That's a good point. I never thought about it like that before.

- What do you think about this?

What they might do:

- monitor and maintain their emotional balance even when plans change at the last minute

- transfer what was learned in one context to a new context

- adjust to new ideas and challenges resourcefully; see new ideas as an opportunity to grow

Now reflect on these questions: When it comes to solving problems on the job, which colleagues are more likely to come up with creative solutions, think outside of the box, and listen to what others think or have to say? You probably chose the ones who are more likely to demonstrate cognitive flexibility about situations, come up with creative solutions, and solicit and value the perspectives of others. To put it simply, these colleagues are flexible thinkers. We define flexible thinkers as people who welcome new information and ideas and think creatively. Flexible thinkers can think about a problem, idea, concept, or situation in new ways and see multiple solutions or outcomes.

Flexible thinkers can think about a problem, idea, concept, or situation in new ways and see multiple solutions or outcomes.

A classroom that promotes flexible thinking—for teachers as well as students—will be a more resilient classroom. When teachers model flexibility in adapting their curriculum, they promote resilience. And when they reinforce alternative ways of thinking about problem-solving for students, they help support students' resilience capacities.

Here is an example of how a teacher thought flexibly about an instructional challenge. During math, Ken planned to begin the unit on fractions but noticed that his students were antsy and a bit distracted. Instead of having the students remain in their seats to complete the assignment from the textbook, at that moment, Ken decided that he and the students would walk around the track and use the laps to talk about parts of a mile. Ken adapted to the circumstances, considered his students' needs, thought flexibly, and maintained the goals he had for teaching fractions. Later in this chapter, we will take a closer look at the ways practicing flexible thinking increases our capacity for resilience and explore how you can support your students in developing the social, emotional, and communication skills that undergird flexible thinking.

Flexible Thinking and Our Social Worlds

We need flexible thinking to deepen our self-identities as well as our social relationships with others. When we think flexibly, we are better able to solidify, modify, or abandon some of the beliefs that make us who we are. We can change our minds when new information is learned.

People who can think flexibly use new information to modify their existing knowledge or dispel previously held beliefs. Recall a time when you were in a discussion with someone who may have held beliefs or viewpoints that were contrary to yours. What happened? Did you hold fast to your belief despite the information shared, did you modify your belief, or was the new information you learned so convincing that you abandoned your belief? Likely, you've experienced all three scenarios.

In social situations, when we think flexibly, we begin to understand and accept that our lived experiences, beliefs, routines, lifestyles, decision-making processes, and culture may differ from others. We learn that there are many alternatives to our ways of being and doing that are just as legitimate as our own. Most times, flexible thinking helps us to get along better with others by prompting us to consider a situation from different points of view. We can put ourselves in another's position and imagine what we would feel, think, or do if we were in that situation. When we see a situation from someone else's point of view, we are better able to understand his or her motives, which can help us check our assumptions and biases and work more harmoniously with others.

Shifting the Fulcrum Through Flexible Thinking

Change is the one constant in life. No two days are the same, and no two children will respond to change in the same manner. Some children adapt to change and maintain their emotional health when faced with a range of challenges; other children fail to adapt to change and experience emotional overload or have meltdowns over what seem to be small changes or requests. You've probably taught children who have emotional meltdowns when asked to work with a different group during an assignment. They cannot adapt, so they become disruptive or shut down because they want things to remain the way they have always been. On the other hand, you have probably taught children who do adapt and maintain their emotions, and look forward to working with a new group.

Children who can think more flexibly are able to see things from different points of view, both their own and the viewpoints of others. Children who think flexibly can reframe a life experience, a situation, thoughts about themselves and others, or relationships from a slightly different perspective. They can even manage disappointments and appreciate alternative reasoning. For instance, a child might consider that there may be a positive, alternative explanation for why he or she was not invited to a classmate's birthday party that goes beyond the explanation of not being liked by his or her classmates. The more we teach children to consider alternative ways of thinking, that is, to think flexibly, the more their fulcrums shift toward positive outcomes in life. We will share how Mr. Clifford Jones, another resilience-informed teacher, fostered flexible thinking in his fifth graders as they learned more about their town's history and its residents.

FLEXIBLE THINKING IN A SMALL TOWN:
Mr. Jones's Story

Eutawville is a small, rural town in South Carolina with a population of fewer than 6,000 people. The median age is approximately 53 years old, and the average annual income is approximately $27,000. In times past, this small town was prosperous. Several factories were thriving, and many people had good jobs in the community. Over the course of the last 30 years, however, nearly all the factories closed, along with many other small businesses, as families had less money to spend. This resulted in more residents seeking work elsewhere and moving away from Eutawville.

At the local elementary school, Mr. Jones, a veteran fifth-grade teacher, often heard his students complaining about how little there was to do in their hometown and how things were better in other places. As a long-time resident of the town, Mr. Jones wanted to help his fifth graders see their community as a viable place with a rich history,

and to understand how and why things had changed. He wanted them to gain experience in planning a project that would ultimately help the community.

Mr. Jones arranged for his students to visit with local leaders, business owners, and long-time residents to hear their stories about what changed in their community and why. He asked every student to identify someone they admired in the community to interview. Mr. Jones also asked students to find older adults who had worked in the factories and ask them about their experiences.

With his guidance, the class researched the town's history. Mr. Jones encouraged his students to think about the stories they'd heard, and he encouraged them to think about different ways to learn about their town's history. Students gathered information by listening to personal stories, reading articles, conducting interviews, and visiting local businesses. They then put together a video

Continued from previous page

presentation for the community, created posters and flyers to post around town to celebrate their town's strengths, and began a monthly podcast called *About the Ville* to broadcast the stories of many of the town's residents. This project was highly successful. Not only did Mr. Jones promote flexible thinking with this project, he also helped his students to understand how to be active and involved in sustaining their town's history and building social connections with people they may otherwise have never spoken to.

Mr. Jones's Flexible-Thinking Fifth Graders

The story about Mr. Jones's fifth graders and their relationship to their small town reminds us that change is the one constant in life. Being the resilience-informed teacher that he is, Mr. Jones understands that flexible thinking is a resilience-promoting capacity that helps children respond to expected and unexpected changes in their lives. When Mr. Jones overheard the children complaining about the lack of activities that their hometown offered, he didn't dismiss their emotions. Instead, he validated those emotions and used that information to build relevant curriculum. The children were encouraged to work collaboratively with classmates on the project. This required them to effectively communicate with one another, consider one another's perspectives, and make decisions about the information they collected. They also communicated with key stakeholders during the interviews and visits to the local businesses. Working on this project also required the students to use their executive functioning skills as they created the video, designed the posters and flyers, and with support, broadcasted monthly podcasts. As a result of this project and their engagement with the town's history and its residents, many of Mr. Jones's students gained a deeper appreciation for their hometown—and their place in it.

Tipping the Scale for Mr. Jones's Students: Encouraging Flexible Thinking

We, too, can promote flexible thinking as a regular part of our daily instruction and interactions with our students in five important ways:

Validate Their Emotions: First, just as Mr. Jones did with his fifth graders, we can strive to validate our students' emotions, even when they seem critical or pessimistic. When a child feels heard and understood, he or she is less likely to dwell on the negative, remain stuck, or give up. He or she is more inclined to find the positive in a bad situation, adapt, and move forward. Better yet, if we can work those emotions into our instruction in a meaningful way, as Mr. Jones did, then we engage our students in learning while helping them build their flexible-thinking capacity.

Model Your Own Ability to Think Flexibly: Children look to us, the caring adults in their lives, for cues about how to behave. If we want students to think flexibly, then in our daily interactions we must model for them what that looks like. Take, for instance, an unexpected, mandated meeting that pops up in the middle of the

day as you're taking students to lunch. Instead of sighing or making a sarcastic remark, we might say, "I really wasn't expecting this. This puts me in a bind, but here is what I'll do to make it work." In this way, the children see how we positively deal with an unexpected event.

Partner With Students to Solve Everyday Problems: When we include our students in problem-solving, we show them that their voice matters and we respect their ideas. The next time an issue comes up in class, let students brainstorm solutions and consider the possibilities.

For example, if we notice that when center work ends, and books and materials are not always returned to their proper places, we might ask students to generate ideas to ensure that books and materials are put back where others expect to find them, and then have them practice a couple of solutions and select the solution that works best.

Provide Opportunities for Learning With and From All Their Peers: Give students the opportunity to work with a range of classmates who might speak a different language, have different cultural practices, or have different perspectives. In this way, we help children to understand that there are multiple ways of being and doing in this world. They learn to take on multiple viewpoints to understand situations differently.

If we want students to think flexibly, then in our daily interactions we must model for them what that looks like.

Let Students Know You Have Their Back: As we mentioned in Chapter 2, we thrive when we have positive, supportive relationships. We can help tip their scales positively when we build the kind of relationships with our students that allow them to trust us, come to us, and ask for help when they need it. This is particularly important for children who are under emotional stress and may have difficulty asking for help or knowing who they can turn to and depend on. As caring, compassionate teachers, we want them to know that it is safe to come to us and we will help them think of solutions to solve their problems.

When the Scale Tips in the Negative Direction

As much as we want to create the kind of environment that encourages flexible thinking in our students, it's not always so easy. It helps to be aware of potential pitfalls, such as the following:

Forcing a Child to Change Before He or She Is Ready: Resilience-informed teachers are cognizant that our actions and inaction can tip a child's scale negatively. We also know that when we think flexibly, we're more likely to seek to understand the root cause of disruptive behaviors before we move to change them. Just like it takes time for a tree to grow enough to be sturdy, it takes time for children to build skills that help them think flexibly when facing challenges. Forcing a child to change when he or she is not ready will not have the desired lasting impact. In fact, it may do the exact opposite, resulting in the child being less flexible, open to learning, and open to our help.

The more children are able to consider different points of view when facing a challenge, the better able they will be to meet the challenge.

Making a Big Deal About Their Mistakes: Another way that we challenge children's ability to think flexibly is when we treat their mistakes as situations to avoid rather than as learning opportunities. When children see things as either right or wrong, or black or white, they are less likely to take risks and analyze the changes they can make to achieve a different outcome. We can alleviate this by creating an environment that welcomes their mistakes and shows them how to learn from them.

We View Diverse Points of View as Problematic: If we allow students to disregard everyone else's opinion but their own, we lock them into a rigid mindset. Children who think they are always right and everyone else is wrong have a limited frame of reference that hinders their ability to face challenges. The more children are able to consider different points of view when facing a challenge, the better able they will be to meet the challenge. This is true of meeting an academic challenge as well as dealing with social and emotional development.

Flexible Thinking in Our Students: Behaviors to Look For

Children who are unable to think flexibly are more likely to break under pressure and not adapt to change—or recover if they find themselves in adverse, unexpected situations. When a child remains stuck in a situation, this has the potential of causing disruptive coping behaviors, such as procrastination, avoidance, self-blaming, or self-harm. These behaviors vary in their degree and intensity and may work on a short-term basis to alleviate the trauma, but long-term use of such behaviors is unhealthy. We want our students to become flexible thinkers who are able to adapt to changes without rigidity. Here are some of the behaviors that we can look for in children who are developing cognitive flexibility:

- They are better able to regulate their emotions.

- They have the ability to think on their feet.

- They can multitask with ease.

- They can solve problems creatively.

- They can view a situation from alternate perspectives.

Promoting Flexible Thinking at Home

Families can support their child's ability to think flexibly, an executive functioning skill, beginning in early childhood by involving them in decision-making. For instance, giving younger children options and letting them decide which outfits to wear to school is a simple way to involve them in the decision-making process. Promoting cognitive flexibility can have an impact on a child's ability to avoid potential pitfalls and recover or transition when there is a disconnect between a child's expectation and his or her reality. When there is a misalignment in a child's expectation and his or her reality, it is important for families to acknowledge how frustrating that may be for the child and to help the child effectively communicate his or her frustrations. It is also important for families to help the child think of alternative solutions to address the problem.

Flexible Thinking in Our Literacy Classrooms and Beyond

A hallmark of resilience-informed teaching is encouraging our students to transfer knowledge from one learning context to the next. For instance, inquiry skills that they might have learned in science exploration can be easily transferred to completing a puzzle during center time. Take, for example, a child trying to fit an oddly shaped piece into a puzzle. With each attempt, the child uses what he learned from the previously failed attempts to make a new hypothesis until he finally selects the correct puzzle piece that fits. The child thinks like a scientist to figure it out:

1. He asks a question: *What piece goes here?*
2. He makes a hypothesis: *It might be this piece with a curved edge on the top.*
3. He tests the hypothesis: *Let me try this piece in the puzzle.*
4. He collects data: *That piece did not fit just right.*
5. He uses the data to refine the original hypothesis: *I need a piece with a curved edge at the top and the bottom. This piece might work. It has a curved top and bottom.*
6. He finds an answer: *Yes. This piece works!*
7. He then asks a new question: *What piece fits here?*

This new inquiry leads him to a new learning opportunity.

Cultivating flexible thinking as a resilience-promoting skill can also be seamlessly woven into our literacy curriculum through the routines and strategies we use. For instance, we might host a debate that challenges students to conduct research to support opposing views on an issue to help them see both sides. We can have children read a narrative selection, identify the problem and solution in the narrative, and propose a different solution for the narrative to generate a different outcome. We might even ask our children to consider a story from the different viewpoints of the characters in the story. Here are a few books that can be used to engage students to think flexibly.

Grades K–2

Going Places by Peter and Paul Reynolds

Rafael can't wait for the "Going Places" contest, where classmates will build and race go-carts. As he works on following directions for constructing his go-cart, his classmate and neighbor Maya finds inspiration from the birds in her backyard. Her unique contraption surprises Rafael, who insists it's not a go-cart. Authors Peter and Paul Reynolds emphasize that not everything needs to be followed like an instruction manual—by combining creative ideas and drawing inspiration from the world like Rafael and Maya, you too can go places!

Good News, Bad News by Jeff Mack

This tale revolves around two friends with vastly different ways of thinking—a pessimistic mouse who often finds himself thinking negatively, and a cheerful bunny with a talent for finding positivity in every situation. In very few words, Jeff Mack highlights the importance of embracing diverse or contrasting viewpoints and encourages readers to extend empathy toward one another.

Sometimes I Kaploom by Rachel Vail

Katie Honors is a really brave kid. She embraces new experiences and new foods despite their strange smells, and ventures into school despite not feeling ready to say goodbye to her mom. However, she sometimes experiences unexpected bursts of emotions—kaplooms! In this comforting story, author Rachel Vail and illustrator Hyewon Yum explore the complexity of children's emotions and navigating the big feelings in our lives.

Grades 3–5

Attack of the Black Rectangles **by Amy Sarig King** In Amy Sarig King's novel, Mac and his friends discover blacked-out words in their school copies of Jane Yolen's *The Devil's Arithmetic*. When the friends discover the meaning behind the black rectangles, they realize it's purposeful censorship from someone at school! Despite dismissive responses and attempts to silence them, Mac and

his friends remain dedicated to the pursuit of the truth, urging readers to do the same.

Love Like Sky **by Leslie C. Youngblood** In author Leslie C. Youngblood's compelling story, G-baby is living in the suburbs with her "blended-up" family, including her little sister Peaches and her new disinterested stepsister. When Peaches falls life-threateningly ill, the entire family faces several unexpected and challenging tests. As they work to navigate Peaches' difficult situation, they discover their inner strength, improve their communication, forgive one other, and build resilience as a family.

Sylvia & Aki **by Winifred Conkling** Based on true events, this story tells the tale of two young girls and their experiences with racist policies. After the bombing of Pearl Harbor on December 7, 1941, Aki, who is Japanese American, is relocated with her family to an internment camp, while Sylvia, whose family takes over Aki's family farm, faces discrimination for being Mexican American. As readers follow the two separate stories, which ultimately intersect, they learn how two young children were shaped by and rose above the unfair treatment they endured.

Summary of Key Points

- Flexible thinking is the ability to think about something in a different way and also to see things from multiple perspectives.

- Flexible thinking is an adaptive skill that helps students understand and manage challenging circumstances.

- Flexible thinking benefits students mentally, emotionally, and academically.

- Flexible thinking is one of the five resilience-promoting capacities of our Resilience Framework.

As resilience-informed teachers, we can create curriculum that encourages our students to think flexibly. In the pages that follow are a few suggested classroom routines and activities that you may use to promote your students' resilience. Many of the routines and activities cut across the four resilience promoting skills: social skill, emotional skill, communication skill, and executive function skill, that we have identified in our Resilience Framework.

ROUTINES AND ACTIVITIES TO ENGAGE FLEXIBLE THINKING

	Routines and Activities	Social Skill	Emotional Skill	Communication Skill	Executive Function Skill	Page Number
ROUTINES	I Get You	●	●	●		121
	Reading Body Language	●	●	●	●	121
	"What if…?"	●	●	●	●	121
ACTIVITIES	Role-Play			●	●	122
	Up for Debate			●	●	124
	Mapping Characters' Emotions and Motives	●	●	●	●	126
	It's a Figure of Speech	●	●	●	●	128

I Get You

Show your students that you understand their perspectives by restating back to them your understanding of what they said or describe to them what you think they may be thinking, feeling, or intending. You might encourage students to use this same strategy to make sure they understand one another in informal and in group discussions. Offering sentence stems like the following can help kids listen more carefully, validate their peers, and work together more effectively:

- "I hear you saying ____. Did I get that right?"
- "That sounds really interesting. Can I say that back to you and you tell me if that makes sense to you?"
- "When you said ____, did you mean ____[restated in your own words]?"

Reading Body Language

Reading body language and using perspective-taking to determine if someone is not fully expressing their true feelings is critical in many social contexts. It is important to both pick up on your students' cues as well as help students pick up on cues that peers share through their body language and then to use that information to successfully engage with their classmates.

"What if...?"

Help expand students' (and your own!) cognitive flexibility by asking "What if...?" questions as a way to encourage cooperative problem-solving and to help students avoid fixed thinking when daily problems arise. Questions like "What if you could eliminate one thing in the world? What would it be?" or "What if a friend started saying mean things about another friend? What would you do?" can be great conversation starters before sending kids off to lunch or recess or as a way for small groups to consider ideas related to a topic or unit of study. Check in with students after they've brainstormed to see what ideas they were able to come up with together.

Role-Play

This role-playing activity helps students develop communication and perspective-taking skills as they work together to portray characters in a scene. They must think deeply about who their character is—What is the character's personality? What is the character's goal? What is it like to live in this character's skin? These thoughts deepen their understanding of the different and unique perspectives that everyone brings to the table, which builds their capacity to relate to others in a meaningful way.

Format: Small group

1. **Introduce students to the activity by explaining that role-play is a lot like acting.** Let them know that they will take on personality traits, express viewpoints, use props, and speak in vocabulary all specific to the character they are portraying.

2. **Select a topic or scenario and describe it to students.** Group students and assign each group to role-play the scenario together. To make the activity more meaningful, tie it to a learning objective. For example, you might cast students as lab scientists as part of a social studies lesson.

3. **Have groups brainstorm to come up with their characters' personality traits, vocabulary, and props.** For example, for scientists conducting an experiment in a lab, props might include a clipboard, petri dish, microscope; vocabulary could include hypothesis, objective, data, results; personality traits might include curious, exacting, brainy. Allow time for students to think about how they will portray their characters in the scenario.

4. Allot a certain amount of time for the role-playing scenario and ask students to begin. Circulate and observe, offering guidance to keep "actors" on track, e.g., How would a scientist start the lab work? What would two scientists say to each other as they work together? How do these two personality types get along?

5. At the end of the role-playing session, you may have students report on or discuss their experiences. Ask students to reflect on how the role-playing activity impacted their learning (e.g., Did playing a scientist deepen an understanding of capillary action?)

Name _____   Date _____

Student Role-Play Rubric

CRITERIA	4	3	2	1
Knowledge of Topic	The team was knowledgeable about the topic and shared all the important information	The team was knowledgeable about the topic and shared most of the important information	The team knew some information about the topic but missed important details	The team did not show knowledge of the topic and missed many details
Roles	The team performed their roles very well and showed deep understanding of characters/situation	The team performed their roles well and showed good understanding of characters/situation	The team had some difficulty performing their roles and somewhat showed understanding of characters/situation	The team struggled to perform their roles and did not show understanding of characters/situation
Language and Vocabulary	The team often used relevant and appropriate vocabulary	The team sometimes used relevant and appropriate vocabulary	The team rarely used relevant and appropriate vocabulary	The team did not use relevant and appropriate vocabulary
Collaboration and Teamwork	The team worked very well together; they respected their teammates turns and listened to them the entire time	The team worked well together; they respected their teammates turns and listened to them most of the time	The team had some difficulty working together; there were moments that they did not respect their teammates turns and did not listen to them	The team had some difficulty working together; they did not respect their teammates turns or listen to them

TIPS

FOR GRADES K–2: You may choose to modify this activity by role-playing as an entire class with yourself included as an "actor." It may be helpful to choose a topic or scenario that students have encountered before so they can better understand their roles. Invite all students at the end of the activity to share what they did in their role and what they learned about role-playing.

FOR GRADES 3–5: As an extension to the activity, ask students to think about multiple ways the scenario can play out, e.g., a construction crew building a new park may run into difficulties along the way. Or you may have each group present in front of the class while other students fill out a rubric you have provided. The rubric may want to address presentation skills, props, and language usage.

Up for Debate

Debates, by their very nature, are a lesson in flexible thinking: Opposing points of view must be carefully thought through and developed. This activity is designed to introduce the concept of a debate by teaching about the pros and cons of an issue. As students work together to formulate their stances, they learn to take one another's thoughts and opinions into consideration, while actively listening and communicating.

Format: Small or whole group

1. **Start with a read-aloud of a text that illustrates more than one point of view about a topic.** Help students understand how one topic can be seen in different ways. For example, you might read *Worst of Friends: Thomas Jefferson, John Adams, and the True Story of an American Feud* by Suzanne Tripp Jurmain and have students consider whose perspective they align with.

2. **Explain to students that debates pit two different opinions against each other.** You might provide video examples of debates between kids on appropriate topics to help students understand the concept.

3. **Introduce a list of debate topics, with clear pro and con sides, for students to choose from, or randomly assign them.** For a simpler approach, you might present one question they can respond to, such as "Should bullies be punished?"

Looking for great ideas for prompts? Check out *Scholastic News Sticky Situation Cards.*

4. **Organize students in small groups based on the topics and sides they chose.** Ask each group to work together to create either a pros or cons list about a position statement.

5. **When students are finished, bring the whole group together and have students present their pros or cons arguments to one another.** Prompt them to listen carefully and to then discuss and rank the strength of the arguments on each side. Encourage students to understand that there is value in different opinions, rather than a "right" or "wrong" position.

They should not be punished becaus
they might be going throug
some thing out home.
They should not be p
because they want to f
have friends probebly.
They probbly dont know how
I dmant care.
They shonld not be
punished becouse they coal
following after some one

Bulies Should be punished
because kids want to have fun.
Bulies Should be punished becau
they might grow up a bad person.
Bulies should be punished bec
everyone should be nice.
Bulies should be punished
because violence is not the an
Bulies Should be punished
because its not nice.

TIPS

FOR GRADES K–2: For a younger group, present one question or position statement to the class. Divide the class into two groups (pros and cons) and hand each team a poster board in contrasting colors (or provide sticky notes to post on the posters). Have students work together on a list of reasons supporting or opposing the statement. When the ideas are posted, invite them to share their three to four strongest ideas with the class. Encourage active listening while you moderate the presentation—you can facilitate by helping them relate their ideas to those of other students, encourage them to provide examples, and emphasize how each opinion matters.

FOR GRADES 3–5: You can extend the activity for older students by engaging them in a full debate. Choose two topics that are relevant to the class or that students can understand (including specialized vocabulary). Divide the class into four groups—two groups will have the same topic, but each will be assigned a "for" stance and the other "against." Invite the first two groups with the same topic to present and have the other students listen and provide feedback on the strength of each argument. Then switch so that the group listening becomes the group presenting.

Mapping Characters' Emotions and Motives

When we help our students analyze the characters in a story, we bring their attention to the different ways people act and feel when addressing a problem—what did the different characters do, how did they feel, and why did they do what they did? By using literature as a model for the real world, we show students that there are many possible solutions to life's inevitable challenges. This kind of flexible thinking can give them confidence in their own ability to weather the storm.

Format: Small or whole group

1. **Select a text with characters with discernible feelings or motivations, such as *The Junkyard Wonders* by Patricia Polacco.** Conduct an interactive read-aloud, pausing to ask students how the characters are feeling. You might pose some "why" questions to get students wondering about a character's motivation.

2. **Model how to create a Character Map. Identify a particular situation in the story that you will focus on.** Write down each character's name in a Character column. Add a column for Actions and a column for Feelings. Model the first example and write what one character did during the situation. Then think aloud to come up with a feeling the character had and add that to the second column. For older readers, you might also add a column to include Possible Motives.

Character Map   Name _____   Date _____

Character	Actions	Feelings
1		
2		
3		

Go to scholastic.com/resilience-resources for a Character Map template.

3. **Ask students to create their own Character Maps.** Have them write what each character did in the Actions column. From there, they can add the character's feelings and motivations, depending on how capable they are at making inferences.

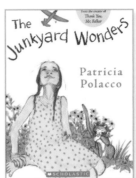

4. **Come together as a class and discuss students' Character Maps.** How did the different characters handle the situation in the story? How could the characters have made different choices? How can our feelings affect our actions?

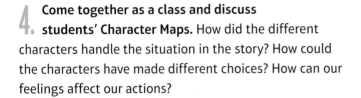

TIPS

FOR GRADES K–2: With the entire class, review in depth the scene you'll be focusing on. Have students create their own Character Maps, only completing the Actions column. Once this is completed, come together as a group to brainstorm the Feelings column. It may be helpful to provide clarifying questions that guide students as they try to identify the feelings and motivations behind the character's actions.

FOR GRADES 3–5: After students have completed their Character Maps, ask them to think about how feelings and motivations are related to each other in the story. As a possible extension, you can focus on real-world scenarios and invite students to volunteer to share an "action" they did, the feelings that arose, and what they were motivated by. Discuss how actions can be driven completely by emotions or by both feelings and thoughts. What tends to happen in each situation?

It's a Figure of Speech

This activity on figurative language, which includes simile, metaphor, personification, and idioms, among others, teaches students to think about meaning on a complex, non-literal level. When we show students that words can say one thing and mean another, we teach them to reframe their thinking, a skill that can be applied in real-life situations that call for managing feelings by rethinking a situation.

Format: Small or whole group

1. Introduce children to the concept of figurative language and let them know that you will read a text with beautiful examples. Select a mentor text with figurative language for a read-aloud, such as *Your Name Is a Song* by Jamilah Thompkins-Bigelow, which features metaphor and personification. Read the text aloud without pausing to discuss so that students can enjoy the cadence of the text.

Kid-Friendly Figurative Language Definitions

Simile: A comparison of two different things using the word *like* or *as*.

> Example: *Before the heat came on, our classroom was as cold as a refrigerator.*

Metaphor: A direct comparison of two different things.

> Example: *Curled up in its blue blanket slept the little white kitten, a tiny puffy cloud.*

Sarcasm: A mocking or sneering remark.

> Example: *A five-mile race after swimming 20 laps? Easy.*

Hyperbole: An exaggeration made to get attention or make a point.

> Example: *I told her that a million times!*

Personification: A way of describing something that's not human in human terms.

> Example: *The wind whispered all around us.*

2. Reread the story and share the book pages or selected text on screen, if possible. Ask students to identify the figurative language found on each page. Talk about the literal compared to figurative meaning of the language.

3. Have students record some of the phrases of figurative language you found during the reread. Have students write or explain the words' meanings.

4. Discuss other ways that people say one thing and mean another, such as irony, sarcasm, and hyperbole. You might extend the discussion by talking about "pleasantries" (e.g., saying you are fine in response to "How are you?" regardless of how you're feeling) and whether or when they are appropriate.

TIPS

FOR GRADES K–2: Have students individually record, in writings or drawings, some of the phrases of figurative language you found during the reread. As a class, come together to brainstorm the meanings of the phrases they recorded. You can help deepen their understanding by inviting students to think about figurative language they've encountered outside of the mentor text.

FOR GRADES 3–5: Extend the activity by asking students to write a poem or short story using the types of figurative language that are found in the book you chose to read aloud. Invite students to share their poems or stories with a partner or the whole class, encouraging active listening. If students are sharing with the whole class, you can also have the class decipher the literal meanings of the figurative phrases in their work.

CHAPTER 6

DEMONSTRATING ALTRUISM

> *Every man must decide whether he will walk in the light of creative altruism or in the darkness of destructive selfishness.*
>
> —Martin Luther King, Jr.

Teachers tend to be altruistic people by nature. We give selflessly, day in and day out. We strive for the greater good as we spend countless hours, on and off the clock, in the service of children. And yes, we are compensated, but the compensation does not compare to the internal satisfaction that most of us feel when we see the lightbulb switch on for a child who has learned something new. When was the last time you experienced the internal satisfaction of knowing that you made a difference in a child's life? How did that make you feel? How does it make you feel knowing that your selfless acts of service not only impact who children are in the present but also who they may become in the future?

When we give of ourselves and help others in need, we are demonstrating altruism. The Yale Child Study Center-Scholastic Collaborative for Child & Family Resilience defines *altruism* as acts for the benefit of family, friends, and community. Altruism is a type of prosocial behavior, a term coined by Lauren G. Wispé (1972). Our internal emotions—empathy, sympathy, and compassion—motivate us to selflessly act to ensure the well-being of another. We are wired to be empathetic (Piliavin, 2009). That is why during natural disasters and life-threatening emergencies, we rush to help one another. This is also why when a child falls or hurts him- or herself, the child's friends rush to his or her side to assist. Altruism can manifest itself in many ways, such as volunteering, donating to charities, or performing random acts of kindness. Altruism is not about doing something for attention, but about doing it with the right intention.

Altruism and Our Social Worlds

What motivates or leads a person to engage in prosocial behaviors such as altruism? Research has shown that we are born with prosocial biases (Celestine, 2020; Brownell, 2013), meaning we tend to want to aid others when they are in distress. Warneken and Tomasello (2009) suggest that young children have an intrinsic motivation to act altruistically. Scholars (Wentzel, 2015) determine that cognitive and affective skills provide a psychological foundation for the development of prosocial behaviors. However, the strength of our prosocial biases varies across cultures and individuals due to differences in genetics, personal temperament, and environmental influences.

Our preferences to help or hinder others are made stronger or weaker through our socialization and the cultural pressures we experience. For instance, if a child is taught to believe that his or her needs are more important than the needs of anyone else, that child will be less likely to engage in prosocial behaviors without an ulterior motive. When a child is encouraged to view a situation from a variety of perspectives or to have a prosocial response, that child will more likely learn empathy and compassion and act accordingly. Researchers (Radke-Yarrow & Zahn-Waxler, 1986) show that children are more likely to replicate prosocial behaviors such as being helpful, sharing, and caring for others the more they observe such behaviors in the people around them. Families, teachers, and other caregivers can help to foster prosocial behaviors in children by modeling these behaviors and engaging children in activities that teach these social skills.

> *Our preferences to help or hinder others are made stronger or weaker through our socialization and the cultural pressures we experience.*

You've probably seen some powerful social benefits from colleagues, families, and students engaging in altruistic behaviors. As social beings, we tend to want to surround ourselves with others who are not selfish or self-centered. Adults and children more often form friendships with people who are empathetic and compassionate and act in an altruistic manner as opposed to a selfish, self-centered, egotistical manner. It is much easier to build stronger relationships among friends when you can demonstrate to them through your actions that you want what's best for them without expecting anything in return. Altruism is the glue that often binds many communities together. Doing good for others not only benefits the community at large but also promotes a sense of community among its citizens. When we freely give to others, we build stronger communities and a stronger society.

Schools are one of the many institutions with an important role in socializing our children. At school, children have opportunities to engage in peer relationships in which they learn and practice prosocial skills. They learn the importance of helping a friend who may find a math problem challenging. They learn the importance of sharing when a classmate forgets his or her snack. They learn how to be compassionate when their best friend's puppy dies. They even learn to understand the views of others when critically analyzing a passage based on different lived experiences.

Shifting the Fulcrum Through Prosocial Behaviors

Children can learn prosocial skills from the time they are born. Wentzel (2015) reminds us that prosocial behaviors have been linked positively to intellectual outcomes, including classroom grades and standardized test scores. She also maintains that prosocial behaviors have been linked to socially competent outcomes, such as being accepted by classmates and teachers, positive self-esteem, and happiness. Positive interactions and engagements within a classroom setting tend to promote prosocial behaviors in children. When teachers promote prosocial

behaviors such as altruism and empathy, they are not just promoting acts of goodness, but acts that are also good for their students' physiological, emotional, and mental health. Acts of altruism can be a great aid in relieving stress, and may also impact a child's peace of mind and increase satisfaction and self-esteem.

Science documents the impact of prosocial behaviors on our overall emotional well-being. There is evidence to support that altruists are happier emotionally. This has to do with the positive feedback loop that takes place in our brains: altruistic behavior causes the brain to release the pleasure hormone dopamine. When the brain releases dopamine it makes us feel good about our actions which, in turn, increases our desire to perform more acts of kindness, and the cycle continues. In other words, the more altruistic we are, the more altruistic we want to be. It is like a muscle that grows stronger each time it is exercised. This is important because empathy and altruism have been positively associated with resilience in both adults and children (Leontopoulou, 2010). Studies have shown that positive emotions have been linked to ego resilience. Ego resilience (J. H. Block & Block, 1980; J. Block & Kremen, 1996) is a personality trait that shows one's capacity to adapt to changing environments. When faced with tragedies, individuals with more developed resilience-promoting skills experience more positive emotional outcomes than those individuals with less developed skills. We adapt best when we forge relationships and deep empathetic connections with others, when we take on someone else's perspective, and when there are lower levels of competition. Empathy and altruism also enhance a child's executive functioning. As resilience-informed teachers, we can help our children develop and practice prosocial behaviors in our classrooms.

Helping your students shift their fulcrum begins with your knowing your students beyond their cognitive abilities. When you know your students on a social and emotional level, you can assist them in learning and engaging in prosocial behaviors that are beneficial. Here are some common characteristics and behaviors you may observe in altruistic students. We don't expect to check off every item on the list for every child, but we can look for ways to guide students closer to these ideals. Children who behave altruistically likely exhibit the following:

- They are helpful, kind, and warm-hearted.
- They willingly volunteer to help out.
- They have high self-esteem.
- They are open-minded.
- They engage with other classmates regardless of their differences (race, social class, language, ability, religion, etc.).
- They are prone to forgive others.
- They tend to forgo something if it will cause harm to a friend or classmate.
- They show concern for the well-being of others.

As a resilience-informed teacher, Ms. Sara Suber understands that life will present challenges. We will share just how Ms. Suber helped her students process their grief about a classmate through kindness for others.

COPING WITH LOSS AS WE HELP OTHERS:
Caleb's Story

Caleb was a student in Ms. Suber's third-grade classroom. He was friendly and always helpful. Everyone enjoyed being around Caleb because he was loving and kind. It was a shock to the other children in Ms. Suber's class when she announced to them that Caleb would not attend school for a while as he began his cancer treatment. Caleb was diagnosed with acute lymphocytic leukemia (ALL), a type of cancer in which the bone marrow makes too many immature lymphocytes.

To ensure that Caleb was connected to school and his classmates, Ms. Suber, her students, and Caleb's family worked with the Children's Hospital to participate in the Bear in the Chair Program, whose goal is to ensure that children, while undergoing cancer treatment, remain connected with their teachers, classmates, and friends. The Children's Hospital sent a stuffed bear to Ms. Suber's classroom. The bear occupied Caleb's chair in his absence. Ms. Suber's students read to the bear, took the bear to activities throughout the day, took pictures and made videos with the bear, and sometimes took the bear home for sleepovers. The photos and videos were sent to Caleb to let him know how much he was missed and cared for, and so that he would know that he had others who were there to lean on during this difficult time. Tragically, the treatment did not cure his cancer, and Caleb passed away.

But the story doesn't end there. This was heart-wrenching and devastating news for everyone at Caleb's school. The students in Ms. Suber's class experienced great despair and did not know how to handle losing a classmate. To help her students heal and learn how to cope with their grief, Ms. Suber created an altruism unit. Ms. Suber was intentional about making space and giving

Continued from previous page

the children time to deal with the loss of their classmate. Ms. Suber read books that dealt with grief, loss, compassion, and empathy. She hosted Socratic Seminars where the children could verbalize and process their pain. She also worked with other colleagues and community organizations so her students could learn how caring for others through their service would also help them with their grief. She wanted her students to understand the importance of their citizenry in action.

The children provided service to people in their school and community without expecting anything in return. They routinely visited the nursing home and an animal shelter, they collected canned goods to be distributed at the food bank, and they raised funds to donate to the Children's Hospital. Ms. Suber knew that their altruistic acts would not only help them heal and remember, but the acts would be the glue to hold her class together.

Connecting Caleb's Story to Resilience-Promoting Skills

Caleb's death was the most traumatic thing that many of Ms. Suber's students had ever experienced. Ms. Suber knew that she had to help tip their scales toward the positive. She used her classroom to do just that. She encouraged her students to work cooperatively and build deeper relationships with their classmates and others in the community as they processed their grief. The children were encouraged to respectfully communicate with each other during Socratic Seminars without the threat of being isolated or bullied. Ms. Suber was highly selective in making sure that the books she included in the unit focused on positive prosocial skills such as kindness and compassion. She also fostered their social skills. Ms. Suber made space and took the time for the children to talk about their feelings and to cry when needed. Each child was given permission to grieve in his or her own way. Finally, she taught the children executive function as they drew up their plans for the bake sale, lemonade stand, and canned food drive. Ms. Suber knows that empathy and altruism are prosocial behaviors worth cultivating, and she makes it her mission to teach this unit each year.

Tipping the Scale for Caleb's Class: Altruism and Our Learners

Losing a friend when you believe that you have your whole life in front of you is not something that any eight-year-old knows how to handle. Ms. Suber is a resilience-informed teacher who took action to cultivate resilience in her students by teaching them how to heal from their pain by being of service to others. She used her curriculum as an entry point to begin showing her students how to manage devastation and loss. As a resilience-informed teacher, Ms. Suber knows that our empathy motivates our prosocial actions.

Ms. Suber is a resilience-informed teacher who took action to cultivate resilience in her students by teaching them how to heal from their pain by being of service to others.

As we saw with Ms. Suber, she created a classroom community built on principles of care, compassion, and empathy. She helped her students learn more than just the academics but also the prosocial skills they need in life. Each time the students visited the nursing home and animal shelter, they were practicing these prosocial skills. They demonstrated their empathy for other children who may have cancer like Caleb as they worked to raise money for the Children's Hospital by collecting canned goods for the food bank. Through this unit, Ms. Suber modeled many important skills such as kindness and care and held them as classwide expectations. Children tend to emulate the actions of those whom they respect. Through her they learned the importance of collective responsibility and collaboration and she taught them that the internal rewards they experienced from doing good deeds for others was reward enough. Doing all of this will potentially help her students shift their fulcrum so that their scale tips toward the positive.

When the Scale Tips in a Negative Direction

Ultimately, we'd like our students to internalize the prosocial behaviors we teach so that they come to naturally exhibit altruistic behaviors. This is best achieved when we model altruistic behavior for them and weave acts of kindness and caring into our classroom activities in genuine ways. Our students are not likely to become truly altruistic if we rely on external rewards or punishments to get them to care for others. Here are some pitfalls to avoid:

- Refrain from offering rewards when children do things that are kind, meaningful, and caring. This can deter them from doing more altruistic things because they begin to expect external rewards as opposed to finding the intrinsic rewards that come from doing good.

- Avoid manipulating student behaviors through excessive praise and bribery. When children are bribed to do something good, they will more often have the expectation that they will only do it if there is a reward.

- If you create a culture in your classroom in which children feel they need to compete against each other for your attention or the highest grades, they will not work in harmony. Competition in a classroom tends to lead to aggression.

Families Can Encourage Altruistic Behaviors

Moral conduct is best learned through actions. Families are the first socializing context in which children learn prosocial behaviors such as compassion, empathy, and altruism (Hoffman, 2000). When children see family members show concern for others, help out a neighbor or someone in need, and advocate for people who are oppressed, this may lead a child to adopt these qualities as well. We don't mean to imply that a child will not develop prosocial behaviors if they do not witness them, but we acknowledge that their potential is greater when they do.

Fostering Altruism in Our Literacy Classrooms and Beyond

Building resilience-promoting skills through altruism in our literacy classrooms will require intentional efforts as we build curriculum. Including a variety of texts and activities that deal with compassion, kindness, and care is a good starting point.

Providing opportunities for your students to engage in class discussions will help them understand each other's perspectives while voicing their own without fear of chastisement or bullying. In your writing workshop, you can have children begin a letter-writing pen pal project with patients at the local nursing home and children's hospital. You can even work with other colleagues to create projects, much like the Kindness Rocks project that Ms. Suber and the art teacher created. We describe this in the Activity Section below. As a resilience-informed teacher, you want to foster prosocial skills in the children you teach because of the many personal, social, physical, and cognitive benefits offered. As such, we highlight how the resilience skills are woven throughout the routines and activities that Ms. Suber incorporated in her unit. Here are a few books that you can use in your classroom.

Grades K–2

Lala's Words **by Gracey Zhang** Gracey Zhang's debut picture book celebrates the power of kind words and compassion for others. In the blistering summer heat, Lala treks daily around the block with a pot of water to visit her "friends": tiny weeds sprouting through the cracks in dirt and concrete. Though she provides them with water, it seems to be her gentle whispers of encouragement that make all the difference.

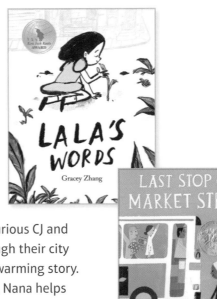

Last Stop on Market Street **by Matt de la Peña** Curious CJ and his wise Nana take a transformative journey through their city in Matt de la Peña and Christian Robinson's heartwarming story. During this bus ride together down Market Street, Nana helps CJ recognize the importance of empathy and the significance of community. With her guidance and support, CJ learns to find beauty and wonder in unexpected places and finds himself eager to uplift his community in the process.

Lucía the Luchadora and the Million Masks **by Cynthia Leonor Garza** This vibrant story about aspiring luchadora Lucía and her energetic little sister, Gemma, determined to follow in her valiant sister's footsteps, comes from Cynthia Leonor Garza and Alyssa Bermudez. When Gemma accidentally damages Lucía's prized silver mask, Lucía becomes frustrated with her trouble-making antics. Their Abu suggests a visit to the mercado to get Gemma her own lucha libre mask, but Lucía ends up misplacing her own among the captivating selection. As they set out to recover the mask and perform an act of kindness in returning a lost kitten to its family, both Lucía and readers discover the most meaningful adventures are those shared with loved ones.

Grades 3–5

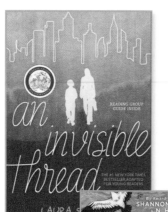

***An Invisible Thread* by Laura Schroff and Alex Tresniowski**
This retelling of the incredible meeting between a stranger named Laura and Maurice, a young boy struggling with poverty and food insecurity, has been adapted to better suit younger readers. Laura Schroff and Alex Tresniowski prove the deepest friendships can spark unexpectedly and a simple act of kindness has the power to make the biggest difference in someone's life.

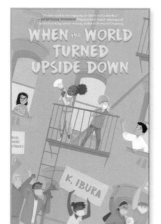

***Flying Over Water* by Shannon Hitchcock & N.H. Senzai**
This powerful novel follows 12-year-old Noura, a Muslim refugee from Aleppo, and Jordyn, a 12-year-old competitive swimmer from Florida who is facing her own personal struggles. Their lives intersect at their middle school where Jordyn takes on the role of being school ambassador for Noura's family following their move to the United States. Together, the girls navigate prejudice in the wake of the 2017 Muslim ban and the enduring power of friendship. Authors Shannon Hitchcock and N. H. Senzai explore the importance of empathy and welcoming ideas and experiences beyond our own.

***When the World Turned Upside Down* by K. Ibura** In a moving tale by K. Ibura, readers are taken through a journey of friendship and resilience during the challenging times of COVID-19. Each character, whether helping care for siblings or mending a lost relationship, provides a unique perspective that highlights the many ways our lives changed during the pandemic. As the friends and their families perform acts of kindness and give back to their communities, readers can witness and reflect on the impact of coming together in difficult times.

Summary of Key Points

- Altruism includes the prosocial behaviors and actions we engage in for the benefit of others.

- Altruism has been positively associated with resilience.

- Empathy is an important motivator for altruism. Resilience develops best when we have deep, empathetic connections with others.

- Altruism is doing something with the right intention and not for seeking attention.

- Demonstrating prosocial behaviors requires that you find the right balance between your needs and the needs of others. You cannot pour into the lives of others if your cup is empty.

Prosocial behaviors such as altruism can be taught. Children tend to replicate the prosocial behaviors that they observe in significant others. As resilience-informed teachers, like Ms. Suber, we can make an impact on the prosocial behaviors we want our children to learn and replicate by using our curriculum as a gateway for doing so. Many of these classroom-approved routines and activities in the pages that follow were used in her room. We describe them and show how they cut across the resilience skills.

ROUTINES AND ACTIVITIES TO DEMONSTRATE ALTRUISM

	Routines and Activities	Social Skill	Emotional Skill	Communication Skill	Executive Function Skill	Page Number
ROUTINES	Think and Act Locally	●	●	●	●	145
	We Can Make a Difference	●	●	●	●	145
	Our Classroom Pet	●	●	●	●	145
ACTIVITIES	Kindness Rocks	●	●	●	●	146
	Supporting a Local Cause	●	●	●	●	148
	Empathy Mapping a Character	●	●	●	●	150
	Text-Based Socratic Seminar	●	●	●	●	152

Think and Act Locally

Have students select a service-based organization that addresses a need in the community. Invite students to research the organization's needs to inform the actions that they'd like to take to help. For example, if the students want to support a local nursing home where patients rarely see their family members, they could think about the things they could do to provide companionship for the residents, such as singing for the patients, reading with them, or even creating arts and crafts with them.

We Can Make a Difference

Have students focus on an issue that they read about. Guide them to research organizations that help address the cause in a positive way. Have them come up with ways they can collect funds or resources to contribute. For example, they could create a lemonade or cookie stand to raise money for families in need.

Our Classroom Pet

Taking care of a classroom pet (puppy, bunny, hamster, bird, fish, etc.) may be just what your students need to learn the importance of caring for something that is dependent on them for their well-being. They can feed the animal, keep the animal company, love on and cuddle with the animal, talk to the animal, and take the animal home on the weekends. Doing this may foster prosocial behaviors.

Kindness Rocks

Creating and distributing messages of kindness is a great way to get students to engage with their community. When students think up messages to inspire community members, they are engaging in empathetic thinking—putting themselves in someone else's shoes to imagine what someone would like to hear. These messages then go out into the real world, which gives students a sense of purpose, knowing that their creation will positively impact others.

Format: Small or whole group

1. **You will need paint and paintbrushes or paint pens, and rocks for this activity.** Gather or have students and families gather medium-sized rocks that are flat and smooth. Explain to students that they will come up with inspiring messages to paint on rocks that they will place around their school or community to spread kindness to others.

2. **Help students brainstorm messages for their rocks.** Students should know that they are creating messages that will inspire others to be kind and give encouragement to those who need it.

3. **Once students have decided on their messages, have them paint their messages on the rocks artfully with decorative and colorful touches.**

4. **When rocks have dried, lead students around a predetermined area, such as the school library, schoolyard, or surrounding neighborhood, and have them place the rocks around for others to find.** Or, they may take the rocks home to give to someone special (they can make great paperweights or bookends).

TIPS

FOR GRADES K–2: It may be helpful to introduce the activity with a short lesson about kindness and how extending kindness can benefit our classmates and our community, asking questions such as, "What does it mean to be kind?" Have students think about their favorite kind phrase to use or one that has been shared with them, inviting them to share the meaning of the phrase if they wish. Then, ask them to paint that phrase on the rock with decorative and colorful touches.

FOR GRADES 3–5: Watch "acts of kindness" videos on YouTube as a class to further demonstrate the crucial role it plays in a community. Discuss how the act of kindness helped both the receiver and the giver. Then ask students to make a Why Kindness Counts poster with two to three reasons why acts of kindness help the receiver and giver. Hang the poster in the school for all students to see.

Supporting a Local Cause

This fundraising activity brings students together to think about the needs of others in their community and discover how to put a plan into action. As students undertake this activity, they will learn to communicate effectively and respect each other as they make decisions together, all in the name of helping others.

Format: Whole group

1. **Invite students to list causes that are important to them (e.g., addressing hunger, supporting animal rights, investing in cancer research, providing disaster relief, and so on) and then narrow it down to a top issue students want to learn about and contribute to.**

2. **Have students research or discuss the issue you've selected as your focus.** For example, "How does hunger affect the whole community?"

3. **As a class, identify local organizations that are working to solve the issue, and choose or have students vote on one that is most closely aligned with students' interests and understandings.**

4. **Then ask students to decide together how they want to raise funds (e.g., by hosting a bake sale).**

5. **Engage students in planning the event (e.g., setting a date, getting the word out, handling and recording funds raised, etc.).**

6. **Ask students to write a letter to the receiving organization.** Students can work on letters individually, in their groups, or as a whole class. You might suggest that they explain why they held the drive, how much they collected, and how they hope the organization will benefit. Be sure that final letters and funds (or collected cans of food) are delivered to the organization. You might arrange with the organization ahead of time that they send a reply to students' letters and contribution. It's satisfying for students to get feedback on achieving their goal and it reinforces for them that their work has purpose.

7. **After the event, talk with students about their feelings about helping others, things that went well, and maybe even some improvements for the next one.**

Students hold a food drive to help stock a food pantry in their community.

TIPS

FOR GRADES K–2: To adapt this activity for younger students (or for a time limit that may present difficulties with involving the entire school) you can focus the event in your classroom and you can consider contributions that are not monetary. For example, if the issue is addressing hunger in the community and you've identified a food bank as the recipient, students may choose to bring in canned goods they already have in their home. Part of the project could be having students find a system and spaces for organizing the donations in your classroom. You can begin to draft a letter to the receiving organization from the entire class. You might guide students with questions, such as why they held the drive and what they learned about the organization.

FOR GRADES 3–5: Have each group take on a writing task related to the fundraising activity. For example, one group can create flyers to get the word out; another can write thank-you notes to place at collecting stations for contributors to take when they leave their donation; others may make posters about the issue and why it needs to be addressed.

Empathy Mapping a Character

An Empathy Map provides a guide for students to analyze characters and their motivations using text evidence and observations through the eyes of other characters. When students analyze a character in this way, they make both observations and inferences, which engages higher-level thinking, including perspective-taking and empathizing.

Format: Small or whole group

1. **Choose a book and read it aloud (or a portion of it) for the class.** You might choose a story that focuses on kindness and empathy, such as *Big Red Lollipop* by Rukhsana Khan or *Waiting for the Biblioburro* by Monica Brown.

2. **Explain to students that we can describe a person or character by the things he or she says, does, thinks, and feels.**

3. **Ask students to choose a character from the story and have them create an Empathy Map for that character that includes space for what the character Says, Does, Thinks, and Feels (or you may supply a template of your own).** You might support students by brainstorming the characteristics of one or more of the characters together.

4. **Encourage students to use evidence from the text to complete the graphic organizer.**

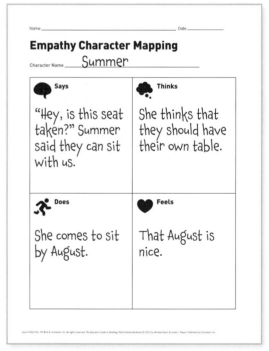

Empathy character mapping based on a read-aloud of *Wonder* by R. J. Palacio. Go to scholastic.com/resilience-resources for a blank template.

5. **Have students share their Empathy Maps with the class, in a small group, or with a partner.** Reflect upon how the four characteristics—Says, Does, Thinks, Feels—give us a full picture of a character. Does what a character says and does always reflect what he or she thinks and feels? Can we use this framework for character analysis to help us understand the people in our lives?

TIPS

FOR GRADES K–2: To simplify this activity, you can assign one scene from the text and focus on a singular character to analyze with an Empathy Map. Have students fill in their Mapping Organizer using the steps above. Once completed, invite them to share their work with the class as you explain that even when we analyze the same character and scene, we may interpret a character's motives differently based on our own experiences.

FOR GRADES 3–5: For older students, group students into pairs and have them create an Empathy Map for their partners to better understand their partners. Ask each student to think of a recent personal scenario he or she would like his or her partner to analyze—what the partner said in the moment as well as the partner's thoughts, actions, and feelings. Invite the pairs to share both scenarios and then create an Empathy Map for his or her partner. If students wish to share their findings with the class, pose questions such as, "What did you learn about your partner in the moment they shared?" or "How can having empathy for others help us be more understanding of our classmates?"

Text-Based Socratic Seminar

When students take part in Socratic Seminars, they are encouraged to create a meaningful dialogue with their peers by allowing all voices to be heard. In this text-based version of the Socratic Seminar, students are asked to discuss a text to reach a deeper understanding of ideas and values by holding a respectful discussion. In doing so, students sharpen their active listening skills and learn to respect each other, which are attributes of empathy.

Format: Small or whole group

1. **Select a text for students to read and discuss.** Choose a text with a complex story or characters that will spark discussion, such as *Watercress* by Andrea Wang, in which the main character goes through a transformation from embarrassment to acceptance and pride. Read the text aloud to the whole class.

2. **Explain to students that a Socratic Seminar is a discussion.** That means they will ask open-ended questions that don't need to be answered. They should focus more on wondering and thinking about possibilities rather than finding answers.

3. **Organize students into small groups, and have each group sit in a circle.** Explain to students that you will lead by asking questions, but their role is not to raise their hand and answer you; rather, they are to discuss their ideas amongst themselves. This shift away from supplying the answer to the teacher requires students to learn to negotiate meaning amongst themselves. To keep a discussion going, students must give time for each group member to contribute, to actively listen to each other, and build off of one another's contributions to expand an idea or offer a different perspective.

Sentence starters to help deepen discussion

- **I agree because...**
- **I also thought...**
- **I also noticed...**
- **I'd like to add...**
- **I had a different thought about...**

4. **Prepare some open-ended questions related to the text.** Prompt the discussion with your questions one at a time. Circulate around the room and monitor the discussions, keeping students on track with reminders to build upon what their classmates are saying. Make sure students are able to express different points of view while they examine what they read.

5. **After the seminar, ask students to reflect upon the process of questioning that doesn't lead to concrete answers.** Help students understand that not knowing can be a good thing—they may be more open to hearing what others think and feel.

TIPS

FOR GRADES K–2: Host a whole-class Socratic Seminar rather than assigning small groups, making sure to choose an appropriate text that students are familiar with. Pose the open-ended questions as you sit in a circle and have students contribute to the discussion. During the seminar, help to facilitate questioning and encourage students to recognize different points of view being shared by their classmates.

FOR GRADES 3–5: Have each group participate in a 10-minute Socratic Seminar in a center circle, while other students are given the role of "observers," fishbowl-style. If groups are reading different texts, it's likely most of the observers will not be familiar with the texts or characters, but if the discussion is successful, observers should be able to understand the focus texts' main ideas and the values the author explores. Once the seminar is completed, invite observers to share what they learned about the texts from the discussion.

CONCLUSION

Given the many challenges (bullying, mass shootings, abuse, suicide, depression, hunger, etc.) that children face on a daily basis, we are convinced that they need our support to help them navigate all of the adversities that may come their way. Students, regardless of their race, gender, sexual orientation, linguistic preferences, socioeconomic status, religious affiliation (or not) all deserve supportive people (educators, family members, administrators, friends, etc.) who are in their corner ensuring that they experience positive outcomes in life. In helping all children build the skills to weather the challenges they face, we not only impact their individual social and emotional health, we also impact our communities and ensure the health and prosperity of society at large.

We know that teaching is not an easy profession. There are far too many things that often steal your joy and cause you to wonder if it is even worth it. But we also know that the impact that one teacher can make in the life of a child is immeasurable and invaluable. So we hope that this book serves as an invitation for you to do your part in making a difference in the lives of every child whom you come in contact with. We are also hopeful that this book offers you practical ways that you can help children meet the serious demands that life often presents. Our hope is that by reading this book you will become that resilience-informed teacher who students will always remember as the one who loved and cared for them when they needed it.

CHILDREN'S LITERATURE CITED

Beaty, A. (2016). *Ada Twist, Scientist*. Abrams.

Betancourt-Perez, J., & Williams, K. L. (2021). *A Thousand White Butterflies*. Charlesbridge Publishing.

Blabey, A. (2018). *I Need a Hug/Necesito un abrazo*. Scholastic Australia.

Byers, G. (2018). *I Am Enough*. HarperCollins.

Carle, E. (1987). *A House for Hermit Crab*. Scholastic.

Cervantes, A. (2018). *Me, Frida, and the Secret of the Peacock Ring*. Scholastic.

Cisneros, E. (2022). *Falling Short*. HarperCollins.

Conkling, W. (2013). *Sylvia & Aki*. Yearling.

de la Peña, M. (2015). *Last Stop on Market Street*. Penguin Random House.

Delacre, L. (1989). *Arroz con leche*. Scholastic.

Derting, K., & Johannes, S. R. (2018). *Cece Loves Science*. HarperCollins.

Garza, C. L. (2018). *Lucía the Luchadora and the Million Masks*. Pow! Kids Books.

Hitchcock, S., & Senzai, N. H. (2020). *Flying Over Water*. Scholastic.

Ibura, K. (2022). *When the World Turned Upside Down*. Scholastic.

Kaepernick, C. (2022). *I Color Myself Different*. Scholastic.

Kelkar, S. (2019). *The Many Colors of Harpreet Singh*. Sterling Publishing.

King, A. S. (2022). *Attack of the Black Rectangles*. Scholastic.

Laínez, R. C. (2016). *¡Vámonos! Let's Go!* Holiday House.

Lee, B. W. (2021). *The Girl With Big, Big Questions*. Beaming Books.

Lowry, L. (1989). *Number the Stars*. HarperCollins.

Mack, J. (2012). *Good News, Bad News*. Chronicle Books.

Martinez-Neal, J. (2018). *Alma and How She Got Her Name*. Candlewick Press.

O'Hair, M., & Sanchez, S. (2021). *You Are Enough: A Book About Inclusion*. Scholastic.

Pérez, C. C. (2019). *Strange Birds: A Field Guide to Ruffling Feathers*. Penguin Random House.

Polacco, P. (2010). *The Junkyard Wonders*. Penguin Random House.

Palacio, R. J. (2012). *Wonder*. Knopf Books for Young Readers.

Reynolds, P. H., & Reynolds, P. A. (2014). *Going Places*. Simon & Schuster.

Rockwell, A. (2018). *Hiking Day*. Simon & Schuster.

Roozeboos. (2023). *When a Friend Needs a Friend*. Scholastic.

Schroff, L., & Tresniowski, A. (2011). *An Invisible Thread*. Simon & Schuster.

Siddiqui, M. (2021). *Barakah Beats*. Scholastic.

Sotomayor, S. (2019). *Just Ask! Be Different, Be Brave, Be You*. Penguin Random House.

Swanson, M. (2017). *Everywhere, Wonder*. Macmillan.

Thompkins-Bigelow, J. (2020). *Your Name Is a Song*. Innovation Press.

Vail, R. (2023). *Sometimes I Kaploom*. Scholastic.

Weill, C., & Basseches, K. B. (2007). *ABeCedarios: Mexican Folk Art ABCs in English and Spanish*. Lee & Low Books.

Youngblood, L. C. (2018). *Love Like Sky*. Hachette Book Group.

Zhang, G. (2021). *Lala's Words*. Scholastic.

REFERENCES

American Psychological Association. (2013). *The road to resilience: What is resilience?* American Psychological Association, Washington, D.C., USA. [online] http://www.apa.org/helpcenter/road-resilience.aspx

Bishop, R. S. (1990). *Windows and mirrors: Children's books and parallel cultures.* In California State University reading conference 14th annual conference proceedings.

Block, J., & Kremen, A. M. (1996). IQ and ego-resiliency: Conceptual and empirical connections and separateness. *Journal of Personality and Social Psychology, 70,* 349–361.

Block, J. H., & Block, J. (1980). The role of ego-control and ego-resiliency in the origination of behavior. In W. A. Collings (Ed.), *Minnesota symposia on child psychology.* (pp. 39–101). Erlbaum.

Brownell, C. A. (2013). Early development of prosocial behavior: Current perspectives. *Infancy, 18,* 1–9.

CDC Vitalsigns. (2019). *Adverse childhood experiences (ACEs): Preventing early trauma to improve adult health.* Centers for Disease Control and Prevention.

Celestine, N. (2020, Sept. 12). *Prosocial behaviors: 12 examples, activities, and findings.* PositivePsychology.com. https://positivepsychology.com/prosocial-behavior/#comment-list

Center on the Developing Child (2015, 2020). *Connecting the brain to the rest of the body: Early childhood development and lifelong health are deeply intertwined.* Working Paper 15. Harvard University.

Copeland, M. (2005). *Socratic circles: Fostering critical and creative thinking in middle and high school.* Stenhouse Publishers.

Daniels, H. (2002). *Literature circles: Voice and choice in book clubs and reading groups.* Stenhouse Publishers.

DuBois, D. L., Portillo, N., Rhodes, J. E., Silverthorn, N., & Valentine, J. C. (2011). How effective are mentoring programs for youth? A systematic assessment of the evidence. *Psychological Science in the Public Interest, 12*(2), 57–91.

Dweck, C. S. (2017). The journey to children's mindsets—and beyond. *Child Development Perspectives, 11,* 139–144.

Espinoza, C. M., & Ascenzi-Moreno, L. (2021). *Rooted in strength: Using translanguaging to grow multilingual readers and writers.* Scholastic.

Felitti, V. J., Anda, R. F., Nordenberg, D., Williamson, D. F., Spitz, A. M., Edwards, V., Koss, M. P., & Marks, J. S. (1998). Relationship of childhood abuse and household dysfunction to many of the leading causes of death in adults: The adverse childhood experiences (ACE) study. *American Journal of Preventive Medicine.* May;14(4), 245–58.

Freeman, S., Eddy, S. L., McDonough, M., Smith, M. K., Okoroafor, N., Jordt, H., & Wenderoth, M. P. (2014). Active learning increases student performance in science, engineering, and mathematics. *PNAS, 111,* 8410–8415.

Green, J., Nelson, G., Martin, A. J., & Marsh, H. W. (2006). The causal ordering of self-concept and academic motivation and its effect on academic achievement. *International Education Journal, 7,* 534–546.

Gruber, M. J., Gelman, B. D., & Ranganath, C. (2014). States of curiosity modulate hippocampus-dependent learning via the dopaminergic circuit. October 2014. *Neuron, 2*(84), 466–496.

Hartling, L. M. (2008). Strengthening resilience in a risky world: It's all about relationships. *Women & Therapy, 31*(2–4), 51–70.

Hoffman, M. L. (2000). *Empathy and moral development: Implications for caring and justice.* Cambridge University Press.

Holt-Lunstad, J., Robles, T. F., & Sbarra, D. A. (2017). Advancing social connection as a public health priority in the United States. *American Psychologist, 72*(6), 517–530.

Kang, M. J., Hsu, M., Krajbich, I. M., Loewenstein, G., McClure, S. M., Wang, J. T. Y., & Camerer, C. F. (2009). The wick in the candle of learning: Epistemic curiosity activates Reward circuitry and enhances memory. *Psychological Science, 20*(8), 963–73.

Kashdan, T. B., DeWall, C. N., Pond, R. S., Silvia, P. J., Lambert, N. M., Fincham, F. D., Savostyanova, A. A., & Keller, P. S. (2013). Curiosity and aggression. *Journal of Personality, 81,* 87–102.

Kashdan, T. B., Afram, A., Brown, K. W., Birnbeck, M., & Drvoshanov, M. (2011). Curiosity enhances the role of mindfulness in reducing defensive responses to existential threat. *Personality and Individual Differences, 50,* 1227–1232.

Kashdan, T. B., & Steger, M. F. (2007). Curiosity and pathways to well-being and meaning in life: Traits, stat. *Motivation and Emotion, 31,* 159–173.

Kashdan, T. B., & Roberts, J. E. (2004). Trait and state curiosity in the genesis of intimacy: Differentiation from related constructs. *Journal of Social and Clinical Psychology, 23,* 792–816.

Kawamoto, T., Ura, M., & Hiraki, K. (2017). Curious people are less affected by social rejection. *Personality and Individual Differences, 105,* 264–267.

Keshky, M., & Samak, Y. (2017). The development of self-esteem in children: Systematic review and meta-analysis. *Psychology Journal.*

Leontopoulou, S. (2010). An exploratory study of altruism in Greek children: Relations with empathy, resilience, and classroom climate. January 2010. *Psychology, 1*(05), 377–385.

Markey, A., & Loewenstein, G. (2014). Curiosity. In R. Pekrun & L. Linnenbrink-Garcia (Eds.), *International Handbook of Emotions in Education* (pp. 246–264). Routledge.

Miller, D., & Sharp, C. (2022). *The commonsense guide to your classroom library: Building a collection that inspires, engages, and challenges readers.* Scholastic.

Muhammad, G. (2023). *Unearthing joy: A guide to culturally and historically responsive curriculum and instruction.* Scholastic.

National Institute of Mental Health. (2021). *Children and mental health: Is this just a stage?* NIMH.

National Scientific Council on the Developing Child. (2015). *Supportive relationships and active skill-building strengthen the foundations of resilience: Working Paper 13.* www.developingchild.harvard.edu

National Scientific Council on the Developing Child. (2020). *Connecting the brain to the rest of the body: Early childhood development and lifelong health are deeply intertwined. Working Paper No. 15.* www.developingchild.harvard.edu.

Nitschke, J. P., Forbes, P. A. G., Ali, N., Cutler, J., Apps, M. A. J., Lockwood, P. L., & Lamm, C. (2021). Resilience during uncertainty? Greater social connectedness during COVID-19 lockdown is associated with reduced distress and fatigue. *British Journal of Health Psychology, May, 26*(2), 553–569.

Piliavin, J. A. (2009). Altruism and helping: The evolution of a field: The 2008 Cooley-Mead Presentation. *Social Psychology Quarterly, 72*(3), 209–225.

Radke-Yarrow, M., & Zahn-Waxler, C. (1986). Socialization in the family, childhood groups and society. In D. J. Olweus, M. Block, & M. Radke-Yarrow (Eds.), *Development of antisocial and prosocial behavior: Research, theories & issues* (Developmental Psychology Series). Academic Press.

Roehlkepartain, E., Pekel, K., Syvertsen, A., Sethi, J., Sullivan, T., & Scales, P. (2017). *Relationships first: Creating connections that help young people thrive.* Search Institute.

Ryan, R. M., & Deci, E. L. (2000). Self-determination theory and the facilitation of intrinsic motivation, social development, and well-being. *American Psychologist, 55*(1), 68–78.

Sethi, J., & Scales, P. (2020). Developmental relationships and educational success: How teachers, parents, and friends affect educational outcomes and what students say matters most. *Contemporary Educational Psychology.*

Shah, P. E., Weeks, H. M., Richards, B., & Kaciroti, N. (2018). Early childhood curiosity and kindergarten reading and math academic achievement. *Pediatric Research, 84*(30), 380–86.

Shin, D. D., & Kim, S. (2019). Homo curious: Curious or interested? *Education Psychology Review, 31,* 853–74.

Sippel, L. M., Pietrzak, R. H., Charney, D. S., Mayes, L. C., & Southwick, S. M. (2015). How does social support enhance resilience in the trauma-exposed individual? *Ecology and Society, 20*(4), 10.

Sutton, J., & Keogh, E. (2000). Social competition in school: Relationships with bullying, Machiavellianism and personality. *British Journal of Educational Psychology, 70,* 443–456.

Tatum, A. W. (2009). *Enabling texts: Texts that matter.* Monograph for Edge: Reading, writing & language. National Geographic School Publishing/Hampton Brown.

Umberson, D., & Montez, J. K. (2010). Social relationships and health: a flashpoint for health policy. *Journal of Health and Social Behavior, 51* Suppl(Suppl), 554–66.

Walsh, F. (1996). The concept of family resilience: Crisis and challenge. *Family Process, 35,* 261–281.

Walsh, F. (2003). Family resilience: A framework for clinical practice. *Family Process, 42*(1), 1–18.

Walsh, F. (2006). *Strengthening family resilience* (2nd ed.). Guilford Press.

Warneken, F., & Tomasello, M. (2009). The roots of human altruism. *British Journal of Psychology, 100,* 455–471.

Wavo, E. Y. T. (2004). Honesty, cooperation, and curiosity achievement of some schools on Nanjing (China). *IFE PsychologIA, 12,* 178–187.

Wentzel, K. R. (2015). Prosocial behaviour and schooling. In *Encyclopedia on Early Childhood Development* [online]. https://www.child-encyclopedia.com/prosocial-behaviour/according-experts/prosocial-behaviour-and-schooling.

Wispé, L. G. (1972). Positive forms of social behaviour: An overview. *Journal of Social Issues, 28*(3), 1–19.

Wynter-Hoyte, K., Braden, E., Myers, M., Rodriguez, S. C., & Thornton, N. (2022). *Revolutionary love: Creating a culturally inclusive classroom.* Scholastic.

Yu, D. (2021). *Life, literacy, and the pursuit of happiness: Supporting our immigrant and refugee children through the power of reading.* Scholastic.

INDEX